Developing Effective Research Proposals

ESSENTIAL RESOURCES FOR SOCIAL RESEARCH

Series Editor: Keith F Punch, University of Western Australia

A series of short practical 'how-to' books aimed at the beginning researcher. The books will cover a central topic, including the main methods, approaches and analytic techniques in social research, from developing a research topic through to writing and presenting research results. Each book is designed to be used as an independent guide or as a workbook to accompany Keith Punch's bestselling textbook *An Introduction to Social Research: Quantitative & Qualitative Approaches* (Sage, 1998).

Developing Effective Research Proposals

Keith F Punch

SAGE Publications
London · Thousand Oaks · New Delhi

SAGE Publications Ltd
6 Bonhill Street
London EC2A 4PU

SAGE Publications Inc
2455 Teller Road
Thousand Oaks, California 91320

SAGE Publications India Pvt Ltd
32, M-Block Market
Greater Kailash-I
New Delhi 110 048

British Library Cataloguing in Publication data

A catalogue record for this book is available from the British Library

ISBN 0 7619 6355 3
ISBN 0 7619 6356 1 (pbk)

Library of Congress catalog record available

Typeset by Type Study, Scarborough, North Yorkshire
Printed in Great Britain by The Cromwell Press Ltd,
Trowbridge, Wiltshire

Contents

Figures

Boxes and Tables

Preface

My previous book, *Introduction to Social Research* (Chapter 12), discussed briefly and in general terms the subject of research proposals. This book goes into the subject in much greater detail and aims to offer researchers hands-on guidance in the preparation of their research proposals. It is based on the same principles as the earlier book – that quantitative and qualitative methods are both required in social research, that training for research should develop an understanding of both, and that the two approaches can usefully be treated together in terms of the logic of empirical inquiry. On this basis, the book deals with the development of research proposals for quantitative, qualitative and mixed method empirical research.

As before, I want to thank the research students and researchers I have worked with over the years. In a very real sense, this book brings together what I have learned from working with them. I also want to thank again Sandra Carrivick for her careful reading and helpful comments and suggestions, Robyn Wilson for clerical assistance, Simon Ross at Sage Publications (UK) for his encouragement and guidance and the team at Sage for their editorial assistance. Nola Purdie and Ron Chalmers both kindly agreed to the inclusion of their doctoral research proposals as exemplars in this book, and I am grateful for that.

As before, too, I would welcome feedback on this book.

Keith F Punch
Graduate School of Education
The University of Western Australia
NEDLANDS WA 6907
Email: kpunch@ecel.uwa.edu.au
Fax: + 61 8 9380 1052

1

Introduction

CONTENTS

1.1 RESEARCH PROPOSALS – PURPOSE AND USE OF THIS BOOK

The research proposal is a central feature of the research world. Typically, the presentation and approval of a formal proposal is required before a piece of research can proceed.

This applies to the graduate student in a university, for whom the research dissertation (or thesis) lies ahead, and for whom the approval of a research proposal is required in order to proceed with the dissertation. It applies also to the application for funds to support research, where the proposal is the vehicle by which the proposed research is assessed, and decisions are made about its funding.

This book is mainly written for the graduate student in the university, but I hope it will also be useful for other situations where proposals are required. Its central purpose is to help students develop research proposals, assuming that the research involved is empirical research in some area of social science. The idea of empirical research is discussed in Section

1.2.1. The ideas of social science, and of different social science areas which use empirical research, are discussed in Section 1.2.4.

To achieve its purpose, the book is organized around three central themes:

- What is a research proposal, who reads proposals and why (Chapter 2)?
- How can we go about developing a proposal? What general guidelines and strategies are there to help students, while recognizing, at the same time, that the wide variety of social science research implies that we should not try to be too prescriptive or restrictive about this? This theme is subdivided into a general framework for developing proposals (Chapter 3), issues (Chapter 4), methods (Chapter 5) and tactics (Chapter 7).
- What might a finished proposal look like (Chapter 6)?

Chapter 2 discusses the idea of the proposal as process, product and plan. Here, by way of introduction, I suggest a '4 Ps' view of the proposal – Phase, Process, Product, Plan.[1] Thus:

- the research proposal is a *phase* of the overall research process – the phase which launches the project, and therefore a very important first phase;
- developing a research proposal is a *process* of planning, designing and setting up the research, including placing it in context and connecting it to relevant literature;
- the finished proposal is a *product*, where the proposal is formally presented as a document;
- that document contains the proposed *plan* for the execution of the research.

This description of the proposal suggests different ways you might read and use this book, choosing the chapters according to your interests and needs. For example, if your main interest is in the process of developing a proposal (how is it done?), I suggest you concentrate first on Chapters 2 and 7, then on Chapter 3, and then fit the other chapters in around these. If your main interest is in the proposal as a finished product (what does it look like?), you might start with Chapter 6, then read Chapter 2 and then the other chapters as required. If you want to focus on the plan for the research (how will the research be done?), I suggest starting with Chapter 3, then proceeding to Chapters 5 and 6. If you want an overview of all of this, you might read the chapters in the order presented.

Section 1.4 of this chapter gives more detail about the chapter plan for the book. The remainder of this chapter now gives some background to it.

1.2 BACKGROUND TO THIS BOOK

1.2.1 Empirical research – data

Our subject is empirical social science research, and developing proposals for doing such research. *Empiricism* is a philosophical term to describe the epistemological theory that regards experience as the foundation or source of knowledge (Aspin, 1995: 21). Since experience refers here to what is received through the senses, to sense-data or to what can be observed, I will use the general term 'observation'[2] alongside the term 'experience'. Thus 'empirical' means based on direct experience or observation of the world. To say that a question is an empirical question is to say that we will answer it – or try to answer it – by obtaining direct, observable information from the world, rather than, for example, by theorizing, or by reasoning, or by arguing from first principles. The key concept is 'observable information about (some aspect of) the world'. The term used in research for this 'observable information about the world', or 'direct experience of the world', is *data*.[3] The essential idea in empirical research is to use observable data as the way of answering questions, and of developing and testing ideas.

Empirical research is the main type of research in present day social science, but it is not the only type. Examples of other types of research are theoretical research, analytical research, conceptual-philosophical research and historical research. This book concentrates on empirical research. At the same time, I believe many of the points it makes about proposal development have applicability to other types of research.

1.2.2 Quantitative and qualitative data

'Data' is obviously a very broad term, so we subdivide data for empirical research into two main types:

- *quantitative data* – which are data in the form of numbers (or measurements), and
- *qualitative data* – which are data not in the form of numbers (most of the time, though not always, this means words).

This leads to the two simplifying definitions used at the start of *Introduction to Social Research* (Punch, 1998: 4):

- *Quantitative research is empirical research where the data are in the form of numbers.*
- *Qualitative research is empirical research where the data are not in the form of numbers.*

These simplified definitions are useful for getting started in research, but they do not give the full picture of the quantitative–qualitative distinction. The term 'quantitative research' means more than just research which uses quantitative or numerical data. It refers to a whole way of thinking, or an approach, which involves a collection or cluster of methods, as well as data in numerical form. Similarly, qualitative research is much more than just research which uses non-numerical data. It too is a way of thinking,[4] or an approach, which similarly involves a collection or cluster of methods, as well as data in non-numerical or qualitative form.

Thus full definitions of the terms 'quantitative research' and 'qualitative research' would include:

- the way of thinking about the social reality being studied, the way of approaching it and conceptualizing it;[5]
- the designs and methods used to represent that way of thinking, and to collect data;[6]
- the data themselves – numbers for quantitative research, not-numbers (mostly words) for qualitative research.

In teaching about research, I find it useful initially to approach the quantitative–qualitative distinction primarily through the third of these points, the nature of the data. Later, the distinction can be broadened to include the first two points – ways of conceptualizing the reality being studied, and methods. Also, I find that in the practical business of planning and doing research, dissertation students very often focus on such questions as: Will the data be numerical or not? Am I going to measure variables in this research, or not? Or, in other words, will my research be quantitative or qualitative?

For these reasons, I think that the nature of the data is at the heart of the distinction between quantitative and qualitative research, and that is why I start with the simplified definitions shown above. But we need also to remember that there is more to the distinction than this, as shown in the other two points above, and that qualitative research is much more diverse than quantitative research, in its ways of thinking, in its methods and in its data.

1.2.3   Relaxing the quantitative–qualitative distinction

The quantitative–qualitative distinction has been of major significance in social science research, and a basic organizing principle for the research methods literature, up until now. Despite that, we should note that the value of this sharp distinction has been questioned in the literature (see, for example, Hammersley, 1992: 41–3), and that there are important similarities between the approaches, some of which are described in *Introduction to Social Research.*

Therefore, once understood, this distinction can be relaxed. This book deals with research proposals for both quantitative and qualitative studies, and is based on the view that neither approach is better than the other, that both are needed, that both have their strengths and weaknesses, and that they can and should be combined as appropriate.

Rather than either–or thinking about this distinction, or tired arguments about the superiority of one approach over the other, the viewpoint here is that the methods and data used (quantitative, qualitative or both) should follow from, and fit in with, the question(s) being asked. In particular, quantitative questions require quantitative methods and data to answer them, and qualitative questions require qualitative methods and data to answer them.

These statements are examples of the principle that questions and methods need to be matched with each other in a piece of research. In general, I believe that the best way to do that is to focus first on what we are trying to find out (the questions) before we focus on how we will do the research (the methods). This matter of question–method connections is discussed in Chapter 3, Section 3.7.2.

1.2.4 Social science and social science areas

To call our research 'scientific', as in 'empirical social science research', requires that we have a conception of science as a method of inquiry and of building knowledge. There are different conceptions of science, but the one I suggest here is very general and widely applicable, has been prominent in the social sciences, and has great value in teaching research students.[7]

In this conception, the essence of science as a method is in two parts. One part concerns the central role of data. Science accepts the authority of empirical data – its questions are answered and its ideas are tested using data. The other part is the role of theory, particularly theory which explains (or explanatory theory). The aim is to explain the data, not just to collect the data and not just to use the data to describe things. The two essential parts to science are therefore *data* and *theory*. Put simply, it is scientific to collect data about the world, guided by research questions, to build theories to explain the data, and then to test those theories against further data. Whether data come before theory, or theory comes before data, is irrelevant. It only matters that both are present. There is nothing in this view of science about the nature of the empirical data, and certainly nothing about whether the data are quantitative or qualitative. In other words, it is not a requirement of science that it involve numerical data, or measurements. It may well do so, but it is not necessary that it do so.

The general term 'social science' refers to the scientific study of human behaviour. 'Social' refers to people and their behaviour, and to the fact that so much of that behaviour occurs in a social context. 'Science' refers to the way that people and their behaviour are studied. If the aim of (all) science is to build explanatory theory about its data, the aim of social science is to build explanatory theory about people and their behaviour. This theory about human behaviour is to be based on, and tested against, real world data.

Together the social sciences cover a very wide domain, and we can distinguish between them in several ways. One distinction is between the basic social sciences (for example, sociology, psychology, anthropology) and the applied social sciences (for example, education, management, nursing). Behind this distinction is the idea that there are different perspectives (for example, individual or group) applied to different areas or settings. Despite the differences, however, one thing that unifies the social sciences is their focus on human behaviour, and the important role of empirical research in the way they are studied. Because of this central role of empirical research, a premise of this book is that there is a great deal of similarity in research methods across the various social science areas.

1.2.5 Relationship of this book to Introduction to Social Research

Developments in the last thirty years or so have greatly broadened the field of research methods in the social sciences. The main development has been the growth of interest in, and the rapid development of, qualitative research methods, in many basic and applied social science areas. As a result, qualitative methods have moved much more into the mainstream of social science research, compared with their marginalized position of thirty years ago. They now sit alongside quantitative methods on a much more equal basis.

In my opinion, therefore, researchers today need to understand the basic logic, characteristics and applicability of both quantitative and qualitative methods. For beginning researchers, I believe a firm foundation of understanding in both approaches is desirable, before any subsequent methodological specialization. It is also desirable that we reinforce the recent trends to move past the either–or thinking which characterized the quantitative–qualitative debate, and towards making full use of the two approaches.

Introduction to Social Research (Punch, 1998) aims to provide that foundation of understanding in both approaches. Its goal is to provide an overview of the essentials of both quantitative and qualitative methods, set within a view of research which stresses the central role of research questions, and the logical priority of questions over methods. In this view, questions come before methods. We concentrate first on what we are trying to find out and second on how we will do it. I see this view of research as pragmatic and robust. By 'pragmatic' I mean that it works, both in getting research started and getting it finished. By 'robust', I mean it works in a wide variety of situations and across many different areas.

Because *Introduction to Social Research* aims to be comprehensive, covering the essentials of both approaches for many social science areas, it does not go into details on some topics. The present book deals with the proposal development stage of research in much greater detail and in a much more hands-on way than was possible in *Introduction to Social Research*. It operates with the same model of research, and with the same view of quantitative and qualitative methods as is described there, but it elaborates and develops issues and points about proposal development much further than was possible in that book. This means there are frequent references to *Introduction to Social Research*, as this book builds on the material there. Where these references are substantial, the relevant pages are indicated in a note at the end of the chapter.

1.3 A VIEW OF RESEARCH

Faced with the many definitions, descriptions and conceptions of research in the methodological literature, I think it is sufficient for our present purposes to see research as an organized, systematic and logical process of inquiry, using empirical information to answer questions (or test hypotheses). Seen this way, it has much in common with how we find things out in everyday life – thus, the description of scientific research as 'organized common sense' is useful. Perhaps the main difference is the emphasis in research on being organized, systematic and logical.

This view of research, which I use as a teaching device, is shown in diagram form as Figure 2.1 in Chapter 2. It stresses the central role of research questions, and of systematically using empirical data to answer those questions. It has four main features:

- framing the research in terms of research questions;
- determining what data are necessary to answer those questions;
- designing research to collect and analyse those data;
- using the data to answer the questions.[8]

As well as capturing essential elements of the research process, I think this view also takes much of the mystery out of research, and enables students immediately to get started in planning research. It focuses on research questions, whereas some other writers focus on research problems. Whether to define the research in terms of questions or problems is a matter of choice for the researcher. The question–problem distinction in approaching research is discussed in Section 2.6.

1.4 OUTLINE OF CHAPTERS

After this introductory chapter, Chapter 2 describes the proposal and its functions, and discusses who reads proposals and with what expectations. It then takes up the question–problem distinction, and presents the model of research referred to above. Chapter 3 provides a general framework for developing proposals, using this model of research and focusing on the central role of research questions. Chapter 4 discusses five issues the researcher may need to consider, which arise because of the complexity of contemporary social science research methodology. Chapter 5 then moves on to consider the methods for the research, and Chapter 6 deals with the proposal as a finished product. Chapter 7 is concerned with the process of developing a research proposal and describes some tactics I have found useful when working with students in proposal development. It also includes two examples of proposals, and points to other examples of proposals in the literature.

Towards the end of Chapters 1 to 5 the main concepts discussed in the chapters are brought together for review, and Chapters 2 through 5 conclude with the questions discussed in each chapter which can help in proposal development.

Two appendices complete the book. The first suggests a way of disentangling the overlapping terms 'perspective', 'strategy' and 'design' in research, and gives some examples of quantitative and qualitative strategies. The second brings together in consolidated form the various questions guiding proposal development which are discussed in different chapters. In this way they constitute a checklist of questions to help in developing a proposal.

1.5 REVIEW CONCEPTS

empiricism – empirical research
quantitative data
qualitative data
quantitative research
qualitative research
science – scientific research – social science
research questions

NOTES

1 I am indebted to Sandra Carrivick for this suggestion.
2 By 'general', I mean that the term 'observation' is broadly interpreted – that is, observation here means more than just seeing. It includes any sense-data.
3 The word 'data' is a plural word, and strictly speaking requires a plural form of the verb ('the data *are* . . .'). The singular is 'datum' ('the datum *is* . . .').
4 More accurately, qualitative research is a collection of ways of thinking about social reality. Whereas quantitative research is relatively homogeneous in its way of thinking, qualitative research is heterogeneous.
5 This is part of what is meant by the term 'paradigm' (see Section 4.1), involving assumptions about the nature of the reality being studied. As an example, quantitative research typically conceptualizes the world in terms of variables (which can be measured) and studies relations between these variables. Qualitative research, by contrast, often studies cases and processes, rather than variables.
6 For example, quantitative research may use experimental designs with measured variables. Qualitative research may use a case study design with unstructured interview and observational data.
7 This view might be described as a 'modified logical empiricist' view, with some additions from critical rationalism – see Higgs, 1995.
8 A modification of this model, to include hypothesis-testing research, is shown as Figure 3.1.

2

The Proposal – Readers, Expectations and Functions

CONTENTS

2.1 WHAT IS A RESEARCH PROPOSAL?

In one sense, the answer to the question 'what is a research proposal?' is obvious. The proposal for a piece of research is a document which deals basically with

- what the proposed research is about;
- what it is trying to find out or achieve;
- how it will go about doing that;
- what we will learn from it and why that is worth learning.

After it is approved, the proposal leads to the project.

In another sense, the dividing line between the research proposal and the research project itself is not so obvious. The proposal describes what will be done, and the research itself is carried out after approval of the proposal. But preparing the proposal may also involve considerable research.

This is because the completed proposal is the *product* of a sustained *process* of planning and designing the research. And both the planning of the research and the proposal for the research are just as important as the phases of research which come after the proposal – those of executing and reporting the research. Indeed, in some types of research – especially those which are tightly pre-planned[1] – the planning of the research can be seen as the most critical phase of the process. In this sort of research, the plan which is developed forms the basis for the rest of the research.

Thus, the research proposal is a document which is a product – the end result of a process of planning and designing. As I will stress throughout this book, it is also an argument which needs to have a coherent line of reasoning and internal consistency.

Two other less obvious, but important, characteristics of the proposal are:

- the proposal is often the first time a researcher (especially a dissertation student) presents his/her work to some wider audience;
- as a finished product, it needs to be a 'stand alone' document. This means that, at certain points in the approval process, it will be read by people who have not discussed the work with the researcher.

I return to these points later. To finish this section, I quote Krathwohl's (1998: 65) comprehensive definition of a research proposal:

> What is a proposal? It is an opportunity for you to present your idea and proposed actions for consideration in a shared decision-making situation. You, with all the integrity at your command, are helping those responsible for approving your proposal to see how you view the situation, how the idea fills a need, how it builds on what has been done before, how it will proceed, how you will avoid pitfalls, why pitfalls you have not avoided are not a serious threat, what the study's consequences are likely to be, and what significance they are likely to have. It is not a sales job but a carefully prepared, enthusiastic, interestingly written, skilled presentation. Your presentation displays your ability to assemble the foregoing materials into an internally consistent chain of reasoning.

2.2 READERS AND EXPECTATIONS

I have noted the two main situations where research proposals are required: the university context, where the issue is approval of the dissertation proposal for the research to proceed to enable the graduate student to complete the honours, masters or doctoral degree; and the research grant or funding context, where the issue is the competitive application for (usually scarce) research funds. Some of this goes on inside universities but much of it happens outside universities.

As noted in Chapter 1, this book is written mainly with the graduate student in mind, preparing a research dissertation. As well as being a convenient way to organize and present the material about proposals, it is perhaps an area of greater need, because several books already exist to guide proposal writers in the research grant context (for example, Lauffer, 1983, 1984; Lefferts, 1982; Meador, 1991; Miner and Griffith, 1993; Schumacher, 1992). But, while written mainly with the dissertation student in mind, much of what is said in this book applies to proposals in both contexts.[2] And, as Kelly (1998: 111) points out, the two contexts come together in the sense that social science graduates will have to apply their knowledge and earn their living in an increasingly competitive marketplace, so that practical skills such as proposal writing become important.

In the dissertation context, readers of the proposal (and members of dissertation committees or proposal review committees in particular) are required to make two sorts of judgements. First, there are judgements on a general level, which are concerned with the overall viability of the proposed study as a dissertation. Second, there are judgements on a more detailed and technical level – such as, for example, those concerned with the appropriateness of the design, or quality control issues in data collection, or the proposed methods of data analysis. This section concerns judgements on the more general level. Chapter 11 in *Introduction to Social Research* discusses judgements on the more detailed and technical level.

The more general judgements centre on such questions as:

- Is the proposed research feasible and 'doable'?
- Is the research worth doing?
- Can the candidate do it?
- If done, will it produce a successful dissertation, at whatever level is involved?

In other words, review committees use the proposal to judge both the viability of the proposed research, and the ability of the candidate to carry it out. It is therefore a pivotal document in the dissertation student's journey. As Locke et al. (1993: xii) point out:

> In the context of graduate education the research proposal plays a role that reaches beyond its simple significance as a plan of action. In most instances the decision to permit the student to embark on a thesis or dissertation is made solely on the basis of that first formal document. The quality of writing in the proposal is likely to be used by advisors as a basis for judging the clarity of thought that has preceded the document, the degree of facility with which the study will be implemented if approved, and the adequacy of expository skills the student will bring to reporting the results. In sum, the proposal is the instrument through which faculty must judge whether there is a reasonable hope that the student can conduct any research project at all.

The four general questions shown above give a sense of the expectations readers are likely to have when they read the proposal, and of the general criteria they will use for judging it. Some implications for the proposal writer follow immediately from those questions. For example:

- the reader needs to have sufficient information in the proposal to make the judgements shown above;[3] the proposal needs to be thorough, and to address all necessary headings;
- the proposal needs to be clear, especially on what the research is trying to find out (or achieve), on how it will do that, on why it is worth doing, and on the context for the research;[4]
- the proposal should show evidence of thorough and careful preparation, even when the research is of the less pre-planned, more emerging kind. Research itself demands a systematic, thorough and careful approach, with attention to detail. The proposal should demonstrate, in its content and its presentation, that the student is aware of this;
- as noted already, the proposal needs to be a stand alone document. This means that it needs to make sense to a reader, often non-expert, who has not discussed the work with the student, and who may not even know the student. The proposal should not need the student's presence to interpret or make clear what is being said.[5]

2.3 FUNCTIONS AND PURPOSE OF THE PROPOSAL

Locke et al. (1993: 3–5) list three functions of the research proposal – communication, plan and contract. This section notes their comments on the communication and contract aspects of the proposal. Section 2.5 deals with the research proposal as a plan.

Communication
The proposal communicates the investigator's intentions and research plans to those who give consent, or allocate funds. The document is the primary resource on which the graduate student's review panel (or dissertation committee) must base the functions of review, consultation and approval of the research project. It also serves a similar function for persons holding the purse strings of foundations or governmental funding agencies. The quality of assistance, the economy of consultation, and the probability of approval (or financial support) will all depend directly on the clarity and thoroughness of the proposal.

Contract
In the research funding context, an approved grant proposal results in a contract between the investigator (and often the university) and a funding source. In the higher degree context, an approved proposal constitutes a

bond of agreement between the student and the advisers/supervisors, department or university. The approved proposal describes a study that, if conducted competently and completely, should provide the basis for a dissertation that would meet all standards for acceptability – a dissertation which should itself be approved. Accordingly, once the contract has been made, all but minor changes should occur only when arguments can be made for absolute necessity or compelling desirability (Locke et al., 1993: 5). This idea of the proposal as contract is valuable, but this last statement needs modification for research which is more unfolding than pre-specified. The distinction between pre-specified and unfolding research is dealt with in Section 2.4 and again in Section 4.3 of this book.

Maxwell stresses that the form and structure of the proposal are tied to its purpose: 'to explain and justify your proposed study to an audience of non-experts on your topic' (1996: 100–1). *Explain* means that your readers can clearly understand what you want to do. *Justify* means that they not only understand what you plan to do, but why. *Your proposed study* means that the proposal should be mainly about your study, not mainly about the literature, your research topic in general or research methods in general. *Non-experts* means that researchers will often have readers reviewing their proposals who are not experts in the specific area.

2.4 PRE-STRUCTURED VERSUS UNFOLDING RESEARCH[6]

At this point, it is necessary to distinguish between research which is pre-structured (or pre-planned or pre-figured or pre-determined) and research which is unfolding (or emerging or open-ended). The distinction is about the amount of structure and specificity which is planned into the research.

To be more accurate, it is really about the timing of such structure. The structure can be introduced in the planning or pre-empirical stage, as the proposal is being developed. Or it can emerge in the execution stage of the research, as the study is being carried out. Across the whole field of empirical social science research, studies may vary from tightly pre-planned and pre-structured to almost totally unfolding, with many positions between. This is therefore a central issue to be clear about in planning the research, and in communicating that plan through the proposal. The distinction applies to the research questions, the design and the data, and it may also include the conceptual framework.

Research which is highly pre-structured typically has clear and specific research questions, a clear conceptual framework, a pre-planned design and pre-coded data. Clear examples of pre-structured studies come from quantitative research – experimental studies, and non-experimental quantitative studies with well-developed conceptual frameworks. On the other hand, research which is not pre-structured typically does not have specific research questions which are clear in advance. A general approach is described rather than a tightly pre-figured design, and data are not pre-structured. These things will emerge or unfold as the study progresses. Clear examples here are from qualitative research – an unfolding case study, an ethnography, or a life history.

These two descriptions represent the ends of a continuum. It is not a case of either/or, and varying degrees of pre-structuring or unfolding are possible. Figure 4.1 (p. 41) shows that.

When it comes to presentation of the proposal, it is likely that projects towards the left hand end of this continuum will be easier to describe – by definition, such research is highly pre-planned, and the proposal describes that plan. Towards the right hand end, the proposal writer has a different (and sometimes more difficult) problem. By definition, the proposal now cannot contain a detailed, highly specific plan. This is noted in the next section, and is discussed again in Sections 4.3 and 6.3.

2.5 THE RESEARCH PROPOSAL AS A PLAN

The proposal also serves as the action plan for carrying out the research. However, as noted above, how tightly pre-planned the research is, and therefore how specific the plan in the proposal is, will vary across different research styles.

Much of the literature on proposals is relevant to research at the left hand end of the structure continuum just described, and shown in Figure 4.1. Thus, Locke et al. (1993: 4) describe tightly pre-planned research when they write that empirical research

> consists of careful, systematic, and pre-planned observations of some restricted set of phenomena. The acceptability of results is judged exclusively in terms of the adequacy of the methods employed in making, recording, and interpreting the planned observations. Accordingly, the plan for observation, with its supporting arguments and explications, is the basis on which the thesis, dissertation or research report will be judged.

> The research report can be no better than the plan of investigation. Hence, an adequate proposal sets forth the plan in step-by-step detail. The existence of a detailed plan that incorporates the most careful anticipation of problems to be confronted and contingent courses of action is the most powerful insurance against oversight or ill-considered choices during the execution phase of the investigation. The hallmark of a good proposal is a level of thoroughness and detail sufficient to permit the same planned observations with results not substantially different from those the author might obtain.

Similarly, Brink and Wood (1994: 236–7) are writing about highly pre-structured research when they say that the plan is all-important, forming the basis for the remainder of the research process, and that developing the plan may well be the most critical part of the whole process. In this type of research, figuring out what you are going to do and how you are going to do it (that is, figuring out the plan) is the difficult part. Once that is done, all that is left to do is to 'do it' – to execute the pre-planned steps.

These comments describe research which falls towards the left hand end of the continuum shown in Figure 4.1. They need modification for those types of research which fall towards the right hand end of the continuum. Proposals for unfolding studies are discussed in Sections 4.3 and 6.3.

2.6 RESEARCH QUESTIONS OR RESEARCH PROBLEMS?

Based on my experience in supervising, I prefer to focus on the concept of research questions, as a generally useful way of helping students to get their research planning and proposal under way. When a student is having trouble getting started or making progress with the proposal, or is confused, overloaded or just stuck in developing it, one of the most helpful questions I can raise is 'What are we trying to find out here?'. It is a short step from this to 'What questions is this research trying to answer?' or, 'What are the research questions?'. This approach makes *research questions* central.

By contrast, some writers tend to focus more on the 'problem behind the research', or on research problems, rather than on research questions. Thus, for Coley and Scheinberg (1990: 13), writing about proposal development in the human services context: 'Proposal writing includes the entire process of assessing the nature of the problem, developing solutions or programs to solve or contribute to solving the problem, and translating those into proposal format'. This approach makes the *research problem* central.

Other writers draw a sharp distinction between question and problem. Thus Locke et al. (1993: 45–51), for example, arguing for 'semantic and conceptual hygiene', distinguish sharply between problem and question, and recommend a logical sequence of problem, question, purpose and hypothesis as the way forward in research planning and proposal development. Similarly, Brink and Wood (1994: 45) see proposal development as building or constructing the research problem, and see research question(s) as one of the central components of that. I think both of these frameworks are useful for highly pre-planned research, and especially, as noted below, for intervention studies, but are less useful for more unfolding studies. In those cases, the distinction between problem and question is not so sharp.

Sometimes social research is concerned with interventions, and assessing their outcomes. Some areas of nursing research are a good example, especially those concerned with nursing in the clinical setting. Behind this focus on interventions lies the idea of a problem which needs a solution, and it is the intervention which is proposed as a solution. This is the logic of the approach to proposal development described by Brink and Wood (1994) and by Tornquist (1993). Writing also about nursing, Tornquist describes research as intervention and action followed by evaluation and assessment. Similarly, programmes and interventions in education or management might be driven by the same logic – a problem requiring a solution, which takes the form of an intervention. The research then becomes an evaluation or assessment of the effects of the intervention.

This line of thinking concentrates on the identification of a problem – something requiring a solution – followed by an intervention or activity designed to solve it, and the research becomes the assessment or evaluation of that intervention. Another, more general, line of thinking concentrates on the identification of question(s) – something requiring an answer – followed by an investigation designed to collect the data to answer the question(s).

In intervention research, the intervention is designed to solve or change some unsatisfactory situation. This unsatisfactory situation is the problem. On the other hand, thinking about research in terms of research questions is a more general approach, which can be used in naturalistic[7] research as well as in intervention research (the effects of an intervention can always be assessed through a series of research questions), and in basic research as well as applied research. I use the focus on research questions as a way both of getting started in research, and as a way of organizing the subsequent project. I think it also has the benefits of reinforcing the 'question first–methods later' advice of Section 3.7.2, and of flexibility, in the sense that students often find it easier to generate research questions than to focus on a problem. But if it helps to think in terms of identifying a research problem, rather than identifying research questions, there is no reason at all not to do so. Nor is there any reason not to use both concepts – problems and questions – and to switch between them as appropriate, in developing and presenting the proposal. In any case, there is interchangeability between the two concepts. Thus, a problem, as something requiring a solution, can always be phrased as questions. Likewise, a question, as something requiring an answer, can always be phrased as a problem.

2.7 A SIMPLIFIED MODEL OF RESEARCH

My focus on research questions, as a useful tool and strategy for developing proposals, leads to a simple but effective model of the research process. When the research is organized around research questions, and when each question conforms to the empirical criterion described in Section 3.6, we have the model of research shown in Figure 2.1.

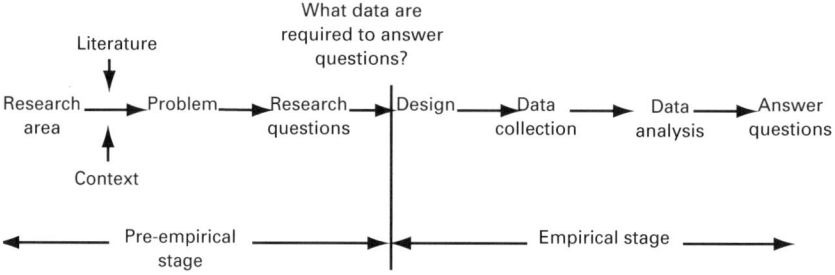

FIGURE 2.1   *Simplified model of research (without hypotheses)*

This simplified model of research stresses:

- framing the research in terms of research questions;
- determining what data are necessary to answer those questions;
- designing research to collect and analyse those data;
- using the data (and the results of the data analysis) to answer the questions.

This version of the model shows research questions without hypotheses. In Chapter 3, we consider the issue of hypotheses in the proposal. Where hypotheses are appropriate, this model can easily be modified to include them. The expanded model is shown as Figure 3.1. (p. 31)

Based on this model of research, we can see that two overall questions guide the research planning process. They are also the questions around which the research proposal can be written, and, later and with some additions, the dissertation (or research report). The questions are the straightforward ones of *'what'* (What questions is the research trying to answer?) and *'how'* (How will the research answer these questions?). Chapter 3 deals with ways of answering the 'what' question. Chapter 5 concentrates on the 'how' question, the question of methods. There is also a third question, the *'why'* question (Why are these questions worth answering? Why is this research worth doing?). This concerns the justification for doing the research, and is discussed in Chapter 6.

This model of research helps to organize the research proposal. During planning, it also helps to counter overload and possible confusion. It is effective with quantitative, qualitative and mixed method research. It needs modification where pre-specified research questions are not possible or desirable, and where the plan for the research is that they will be developed as the early empirical work provides focus. In those cases, it is still worth keeping this model in mind, in order to see where and why it is inappropriate. When research questions are developed as the research becomes focused, the analytic process is delayed. It comes during and after some empirical work, not before. When that happens, development of the research questions will be influenced by insights and trends emerging from the initial data. Otherwise, it is much the same process, and just as important for ensuring the fit between the parts of the research. This model is also effective with research conceptualized in terms of problems rather than questions. If the research is the assessment of an intervention designed as a solution to some problem, the assessment or evaluation can easily be structured as a series of research questions.

2.8 REVIEW CONCEPTS AND QUESTIONS

Concepts research proposal the proposal as: *plan* *product* *process* *phase* pre-structured research unfolding research research questions research problems

Questions • Who will read my proposal? • What will their expectations be? • What is the process for approval of my proposal? • What departmental and/or university guidelines are there for my proposal and its presentation?

NOTES

1 See Section 2.4.
2 At the same time, there are differences between them, and special aspects and emphases in the way proposals are prepared and presented in the two contexts. Examples are the much more detailed budgetary information (including justification), the more prescribed format and more detailed work plan and time line usually required in the grant situation.

3 A very unfortunate reaction from a proposal reviewer is: 'I don't find enough information in this proposal to make judgements'.

4 An equally unfortunate reaction is 'I can't understand this proposal, it is not clear'.

5 I single this point out because of the frequency with which I find it occurs in research supervision. I am sure every supervisor is familiar with the following exchange:

> *Supervisor* (reacting, for example, to a proposal draft): 'This is not clear', or 'I cannot understand this'.
> *Student* (in response): 'What I meant was . . .' and proceeds to clarify.

The point is, of course, that the student will usually not be there to clarify what is written when the committee member is reading the proposal, or when a wider audience is involved. It is necessary to make the proposal clear in the 'stand alone' sense.

6 See *Introduction to Social Research*, (Punch, 1988) pp. 25–7.

7 'Naturalistic' refers here to research which does not contrive or manipulate the situation, and which does not involve any intervention or treatment. It studies the world 'as it is'.

3

A General Framework for Developing Proposals

CONTENTS

This chapter describes a general framework for developing and organizing research proposals, focusing on the central role of research questions. While this description has organization and structure, this does not mean that developing a proposal does (or should) proceed in the tidy, organized, deductive way that it might seem to imply. It is possible for a proposal to develop in this way. But it is more likely that its development will be a messy, cyclical process, with hesitations and frustrations, where the researcher cycles backwards and forwards between different issues and different sections, iterating towards a final version. This echoes the process–product distinction noted in Chapter 2. The process is untidy, but the product is (expected to be) neat, well-structured and easy to follow.

3.1 AN OVERALL FRAMEWORK

Chapter 2 suggested that the proposal must deal with these main themes:

- what the proposed research is about;
- what it is trying to find out or achieve;
- how it will go about doing that;
- what we will learn from that and why it is worth learning.

As shown in discussing the model of research just presented, we can now represent these themes in three general but central questions, which the proposal needs to answer:

- What?
- How?
- Why?

Irrespective of the position a researcher takes on the issues raised in the next chapter, these three general questions are at the heart of the proposal. Together they form an overall framework for its development.

- *'What'* means what this research is trying to find out (or do, or achieve). Phrased this way, it points directly to research questions, first general and then specific.
- *'How'* means how the research proposes to answer its questions. Answering the 'how' question means dealing with the methods of the research. Methods are seen here as dependent on research questions.
- *'Why'* means why this research is worth doing. This points to the justification (or significance, or importance, or contribution) of the research. It acknowledges that all research requires the investment of considerable time, energy and other resources, and it asks for justification of that investment. It also involves the idea of the proposal (and research) as a coherent argument. To some extent, the argument presented in the proposal should itself answer the question of why the research is worth doing. In addition, as shown in Chapter 6, there may well be another section in the proposal which addresses explicitly the justification or contribution of the research.

In line with the argument of *Introduction to Social Research* (Punch, 1998), reinforced here in Section 3.7.2 – that, generally speaking, a good way to proceed is to work on 'what' before 'how' – this chapter concentrates on research questions. Putting the 'what' before the 'how' means putting questions before methods. Methods are dealt with in this book in Chapter 5.

3.2 A HIERARCHY OF CONCEPTS[1]

One advantage of planning research in terms of research questions is that it makes explicit the idea of levels of abstraction in research. We can distinguish five levels of concepts and questions, which vary in levels of abstraction, forming an inductive–deductive hierarchy:[2]

- research area;
- research topic;
- general research question(s);
- specific research question(s);
- data collection question(s).

To say these five things form a hierarchy is to say that they vary systematically in levels of abstraction and generality, and that they need to be connected to each other logically, by induction and deduction, across those levels. The top level is the most general and the most abstract. The bottom level is the most specific and the most concrete.

Thus, from the top down, the research area is more general than the research topic, which itself is more general than the general research question(s), which are more general than the specific research questions, which in turn are more general than the data collection questions.

Another way of saying this, and now moving from the bottom up, is that the data collection questions are implied by, or are included in, or follow on from, the specific research questions, which in turn are implied by or included in or follow on from the general research questions, and so on up the hierarchy.

A benefit of thinking this way, and of organizing research this way, is that it exposes and highlights the links between these various levels of abstraction. It is necessary to have tight logical links between these levels for the research to have internal consistency, coherence and validity. This is what is meant by 'follow on from' in the paragraph above. The technical concepts involved here are deduction and induction. We move downwards in the hierarchy by deduction, and upwards by induction.

Not all research projects can be organized or planned this way. In particular, those which have a more unfolding design would not fit easily with this well-pre-structured approach. There are also issues about 'generalizing' vs 'particularizing' research questions (Maxwell, 1996: 54–5),[3] and the intended emphasis on one of these types of question or the other in a particular study. But, having noted that, many projects do fit well into this approach, and, in any case, this hierarchy of concepts is useful both pedagogically and practically. Not only does thinking in these terms help to organize the developing proposal. It also helps you to communicate clearly about your research, and to write the proposal (and, later on, the dissertation). And if a study emphasizes particularizing question(s), working through these levels of abstraction helps to sharpen its logic and to strengthen its internal validity.

3.3 RESEARCH AREAS AND TOPICS

Research areas are usually stated in a few words, and sometimes just one word. Topics similarly are a few words, but usually more than those describing the research area. The topic falls within the area. It is an aspect, or part, of the area, a step towards making the general area more specific. It is included in the area, but it is, of course, not the only topic within the area.

Examples of research areas are absenteeism at work, youth culture in high schools, living with Tourette's Syndrome, academic success and failure at university, membership of voluntary organizations, and youth suicide. Four possible research topics within the research area youth suicide are shown in Box 3.1.

Identifying first the research area, and then the topic within the area, immediately gives a first level of focus to the research, a first narrowing of the possibilities. Of course, any research area includes many topics, so two decisions are involved here – the first is the selection of an area, the second is the selection of a topic within the area. Many times, students have not so much difficulty with the first decision, the area. They know generally what research area they are interested in. Often, they have rather more difficulty with the second decision: With all these possible topics within this area, which should I choose?

A valuable consequence of identifying the research area is that it enables you as the researcher immediately to connect your work to the literature. It defines a body of literature as relevant to this piece of research. Identifying a topic within an area gives still-more-specific direction to the

BOX 3.1 *From research area to research topics*

Research area: youth suicide
Four possible research topics:

1. Suicide rates among different groups
2. Factors associated with the incidence of youth suicide
3. Managing suicide behaviour among teenagers
4. Youth culture and the meaning of suicide

Note: Topics 1 and 2 imply a predominantly quantitative approach. Topics 3 and 4 imply a predominantly qualitative approach

literature. It enables a more specific body of literature to be identified as centrally relevant to the research.

3.4 GENERAL AND SPECIFIC RESEARCH QUESTIONS

General and specific research questions bring things down to the next level of specificity, further narrowing the focus of the proposed research. The distinction between them is in terms of specificity. General research questions are more general, more abstract, and (usually) are not themselves directly answerable, because they are too general. Specific research questions are more specific, detailed and concrete. They are directly answerable because they point directly at the data needed to answer them. This last point is elaborated in Section 3.6.

Just as there are many research topics within a research area, so there are many possible general research questions within a research topic. Specific research questions take the deductive process further, subdividing a general question into the specific questions which follow from it.

A general question is normally too broad to be answered directly, and too broad to satisfy the empirical criterion (see Section 3.6). Its concepts are too general. It therefore requires subdivision into several specific research questions. The general research question is answered indirectly by accumulating and integrating the answers to the corresponding specific research questions. A study may well have more than one general research question. In that case, each will require analysis and subdivision into appropriate specific research questions. Boxes 3.2 and 3.3 illustrate this process with the research area of youth suicide, and the topic of factors associated with the incidence of youth suicide.

BOX 3.2   *From research topic to general research questions*

Research topic: factors associated with the incidence of youth suicide

- General research question 1:   What is the relationship between family background factors and the incidence of youth suicide?

- General research question 2:   What is the relationship between school experience factors and the incidence of youth suicide?

Note: More general research questions are possible. These are only two examples. As noted in Box 3.1, this topic and these general questions have a quantitative bias.

BOX 3.3   *From general research question to specific research questions*

General research question: What is the relationship between family
                         background factors and the incidence of
                         youth suicide?

- Specific research question 1:

  - What is the relationship between family income and the incidence
    of youth suicide?
    Or
  - Do youth suicide rates differ between families of different income
    levels?

- Specific research question 2:

  - What is the relationship between parental break-up and the
    incidence of youth suicide?
    Or
  - Do youth suicide rates differ between families where parents are
    divorced or separated, and families where they are not?

Note: More-specific research questions are possible. These are only two
examples.

This distinction is really a matter of common sense, and, in the practical business of planning research, is not difficult to make. And, as already noted, while the description here is presented deductively, it is by no means necessary for things to proceed that way. They may also proceed inductively, and, as is probably most common, by some cyclical and iterative mixture of induction and deduction.

In formal terms, a good way to distinguish general from specific research questions is to apply the empirical criterion below (Section 3.6) to each question, as it is developed: Is it clear what data will be required to answer this question? If the answer for each question is yes, we can proceed from questions to methods. If the answer is no, one thing probably needed is further specificity. This criterion is also a good check on deciding whether we have reached a set of researchable questions.

At the heart of this discussion is the process of making a general concept more specific by showing its dimensions, aspects, factors, components, or indicators. In effect, you are defining a general concept 'downwards' towards its data indicators. Of the several terms shown above (dimensions, aspects, factors, components, indicators), I prefer the term *indicators* because of its wide applicability across different types of research. It applies in quantitative and qualitative contexts, whereas the terms 'dimensions', 'factors' and 'components' have more quantitative connotations.

A proviso, more likely to be needed in qualitative studies, is that the research may proceed upwards in abstraction from indicators to general concepts, rather than downwards in abstraction from general concepts to indicators. To repeat, the important thing is not which way the research proceeds. You can proceed downwards, using deduction, from general concept to specific concept to indicators, or you can proceed upwards, using induction, from indicators to specific and general concepts. Or deduction and induction can both be used. The important thing is that the finished product as a proposal (and, ultimately, as a piece of research), shows logical connections across the different levels of abstraction.

3.5 DATA COLLECTION QUESTIONS

At the lowest level in this hierarchy come data collection questions. They are the most specific level of questions.

The reason for noting and separating out data collection questions here is that students sometimes confuse research questions with data collection questions. A research question is a question the research itself is trying to answer. A data collection question is a question which is asked in order to collect data in order to help answer the research question. In that sense, it is more specific still than the research question. In that sense too, more than one data collection question, sometimes several and sometimes many, will be involved in assembling the data necessary to answer one research question.[4]

What does this hierarchy of concepts mean for proposal development? I have gone into this detailed analysis because it is often a central aspect of the pre-empirical, setting-up stage of the research, and because it shows clearly the differing levels of abstraction. Understanding this hierarchy of concepts is important, but it is unlikely to be applicable, formula-like, in proposal development. As already noted, the question development stage is likely to be messy, iterative and cyclical, and it can proceed any way at all.[5] But if you are aware of this hierarchy, you can use it to help disentangle and organize the many questions which serious consideration of almost any research area and topic will produce.

3.6 RESEARCH QUESTIONS AND DATA – THE EMPIRICAL CRITERION[6]

In empirical research, it is necessary that data be linked to concepts and concepts to data, and that the links between concepts and data be tight, logical and consistent. This idea needs to be applied to our research questions.

Concepts are embedded in research questions. General questions use general concepts, and specific questions use specific concepts. General concepts are typically too general and abstract to be linked directly to data indicators. Rather, they are linked indirectly to data through specific concepts. Translating general concepts down to specific concepts means specifying what the researcher will take to be indicators, in the empirical data, of these concepts.

The idea of the empirical criterion for research questions is that a well-developed and well-stated research question indicates what data will be necessary to answer it. It is the idea behind the expression that 'a question well asked is a question half answered'. This idea was illustrated in *Introduction to Social Research* (Punch, 1988: 46) using an example from educational research. That example shows the research question phrased at a sufficient level of specificity that we can see what data we will require in order to answer it.

We can routinely apply this empirical criterion to research questions as they are developed. For each question, is it clear what data will be required to answer the question? If the research questions do not give clear indications of the data needed to answer them, we will not know how to proceed in the research when it comes to the data collection and analysis stages.[7]

One common example of this concerns 'should' questions, which arise frequently when students are first planning research. It is worth looking at this in some detail, both because it illustrates the point being made in this section, and because it arises frequently. By 'should' questions, I mean such questions as:

- Should teachers assess students? Should teachers know the IQ of students? Should teachers use corporal punishment?
- Should nurses wear white uniforms? Should nurses allow patients to participate in care planning? (Brink and Wood, 1994: 8)
- Should managers use democratic or authoritarian leadership styles? Should organizations have a flat structure or a hierarchical structure?

Such questions are complex, not least because they involve (or appear to involve) a value judgement. But, for our purposes in this section, these questions fail the test of the empirical criterion. Thus, for any of these 'should' questions, it is not clear what data would be required to answer it. Therefore, such questions are not researchable or answerable with data, as stated. They are not empirical questions, as they stand, and need rephrasing if they are to be answered by empirical research.

I am not saying that these are unimportant questions. On the contrary, a strong argument can be made that 'should' questions are among the most important type of questions that we need to answer. I am only saying that they are not empirical questions, as phrased, and therefore they need either to be answered using methods which are not empirical, or to be rephrased.

Usually such questions can be rephrased, to make them answerable empirically. There are different ways this can be done. One simple way, which is often helpful, is to rephrase using 'Does X think that . . .' (where X needs to be defined). Thus: 'Should nurses wear white uniforms?' might become:

- Do nurses think they should wear white uniforms? Or,
- Do hospital administrators think nurses should wear white uniforms? Or,
- Do patients think nurses should wear white uniforms? And so on.

These rephrased questions now start to meet the empirical criterion. Thus, the first rephrasing clearly indicates that we will need data from nurses about their views on the wearing of white uniforms.[8] The second shows we will need similar data from hospital administrators, and so on.

To sum up, as you develop your research questions, ask, for each question 'What data are needed to answer this question?'.

3.7 THREE TACTICAL ISSUES

Chapter 7 deals with some general and specific tactics in developing a proposal. In addition to that discussion, three tactical issues are noted here, because they fit in well with the content of this chapter. They are:

- the importance of the pre-empirical stage of research;
- questions before methods;
- do I need hypotheses?

3.7.1 The importance of the pre-empirical stage

The pre-empirical stage of research refers to the issues discussed in this chapter, and also in chapter 4 of this book. I use the term 'question development' to describe this stage of the analysis and development of the research questions. In my opinion, it is just as important as the empirical or methods stage of the research. It is really where things are set up, and it therefore has an important determining influence on what is done later – although, naturally, that influence is more important in pre-structured than in unfolding studies. But its importance is not very often stressed in the research methods literature. I think that has been partly because of the preoccupation in the field with methodological issues. Of course, I do not say that these methodological issues are unimportant. Rather, I want to counterbalance them by stressing the importance of the question development and conceptual analysis work required in the pre-empirical stage. A crucial step in this pre-empirical work is the selection and identification of research area and topic. Once these decisions are clear in the research student's mind, a great deal has been achieved.

3.7.2 Questions before methods[9]

Questions and methods need to be aligned with each other in a piece of research. This is part of the internal validity of a piece of research, and is more important than ever in social science research today, where quantitative and qualitative methods sit alongside each other, and may be combined in the one study.

In general, the best way to achieve this alignment is to focus first on developing the research questions, and second on methods to answer those questions. 'In general' in this sentence means that there are exceptions to this order of events, and that it is not mandatory. But I recommend it because I have found that a common difficulty for research students is to worry about issues of method in advance of getting a clear view of the research questions. Too often, a student wants to ask, too early, 'How will I do my research?' or 'Can I use such and such a method?'. Those questions of course have their place. But that place is not so early in the process of planning the research that they come before the substantive issues dealing with what the research is trying to find out.

3.7.3 Do I need hypotheses in my proposal?[10]

On a much more specific level, I single out the question 'Do I need hypotheses?' because I find it comes up frequently, and causes confusion. In a nutshell, I believe that hypotheses should be used in research as and when appropriate, rather than in some mandatory or automatic way. That belief is based on the view that hypotheses have an important function in research when they can be deduced from a theory, or when they are explained by a theory, so that the research, in testing the hypotheses, is really testing the theory behind the hypotheses.

This is the 'classical' or traditional hypothetico-deductive view of research, and it has its place and its importance. But not all social research does or should align itself with this model. As the reasoning in *Introduction to Social Research* (Punch, 1988) tries to make clear, there are two straightforward questions which can help in determining whether hypotheses are appropriate in a particular study:

- for each specific research question, can I predict (in advance of the empirical research – that is, in advance of getting and analysing the data) what I am likely to find?

- if so, is the basis for that prediction a rationale, some set of propositions, a 'theory' from which the hypotheses follow, and which 'explains' the hypotheses?

If so, I should by all means formulate and test hypotheses in the research, and, in so doing, test the theory. If not, I suggest we leave the matter at the level of research questions. I can see no logical difference between answering research questions and testing hypotheses, when it comes to what data we will get and how we will analyse them. The same operations are required.

This question (hypotheses or no hypotheses?) does not have to be a strict either–or matter. The idea of the 'guiding hypothesis' is often useful in research. This may be an informed guess or hunch, for which the researcher does not yet have a fully developed rationale as described above. As well as bringing together, summarizing and integrating the researcher's thinking on the topic, which is valuable, such a guiding hypothesis can also give structure to the design, data collection and data analysis aspects of the study, and can expose other concepts in the researcher's thinking. In that sense, it is useful. But we should remember that research questions can do these functions as well. In particular, the sometimes noted 'focusing' function of a hypothesis is just as well fulfilled by a research question.

In short, I am against the idea that we should have hypotheses in research proposals *just for the sake of having hypotheses*. Let us use them if appropriate, and not use them if not appropriate. Figure 2.1 showed a model of research built around research questions. This model can be modified for research which sets out to test hypotheses. The modified model is shown in Figure 3.1

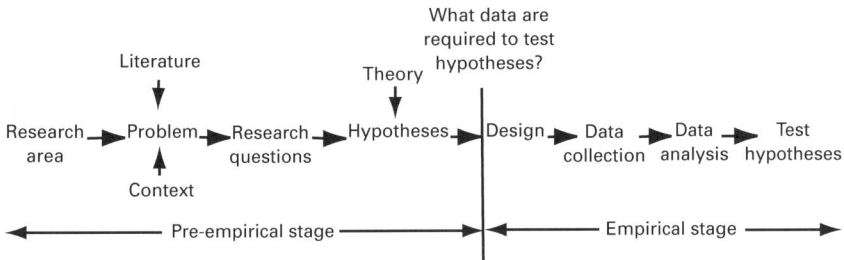

FIGURE 3.1   *Simplified model of research (with hypotheses)*

3.8 REVIEW CONCEPTS AND QUESTIONS

Concepts

research area
research topic
general research question(s)
specific research question(s)
data collection questions
empirical criterion
hypotheses – relationship to theory

Questions

At the most general level:

- What – What is my research about?
  - What is its purpose?
  - What is it trying to find out or achieve?
especially:
  - What questions is it trying to answer?
- How – How will my research answer its questions?
- Why – Why is this research worth doing?

More specifically:

- What is my research area? Have I clearly identified it?
- What is my topic? Have I clearly identified it and shown how it fits within the research area?
- What are my general research questions?
- What are my specific research questions?
- Does each specific research question meet the empirical criterion? Is it clear what data are required to answer each question?

NOTES

1 See *Introduction to Social Research* (Punch, 1998), pp. 33–9, 46–9.
2 This extends the three-level hierarchy noted in *Introduction to Social Research* (Punch, 1988: 34) – research area, general research questions, specific research questions.

3 This distinction is similar to the nomothetic–idiographic distinction (see Punch, 1988: 18, 31). A generalizing question seeks nomothetic knowledge – universalized, law-like statements applying generally across a class of people, situations, events, or phenomena. A particularizing question seeks idiographic knowledge – local, case-based, specific propositions.

4 This does not apply literally to all actual data collection questions which might be used in a study. Thus some data collection questions might themselves be quite general questions – for example, introductory or 'grand tour' questions in a qualitative research interview. But the point being made here is that the role of most data collection questions in the research is to operate at the most specific level. As Maxwell (1996: 53) says, research questions identify what you want to understand; interview questions, as data collection questions, provide the data you need to understand these things. The same is true of survey questions. Being the most specific level of questions, the actual data collection questions may well not be shown in the proposal.

5 Locke et al. (1993) give examples of this question development process, including inductively (p. 50) and deductively (p. 53). Maxwell (1996: 54–9), writing for qualitative research, makes distinctions between research questions (generalizing–particularizing, instrumentalist–realist, variance–process). He also (p. 50) gives an example of the development of research questions, and (pp. 61–2) gives an exercise to assist in this. Madsen (1983: 30–4) shows how to develop subsidiary (that is, specific) research questions from a general question.

6 See *Introduction to Social Research* (Punch, 1988), pp. 46–55.

7 Writing specifically for nursing research, Brink and Wood (1994: 5–18) come at this same idea when they write about 'researchable' questions – ones that yield 'hard facts'. Their book includes a discussion of the sources, components and types of researchable questions, and an extended discussion of levels of questions. They also write about turning 'should' questions into 'action' questions (p. 8).

8 The rephrasing needs to go further than just this, for the question to meet the empirical criterion completely. Also, of course, there are other ways of rephrasing the original 'should' question. This simple way has been used for illustration, but this way of rephrasing might well be part of any evaluative answer to the original question, even though it changes its meaning somewhat. Another way is to rephrase the 'should' question in terms of means–ends (or causes–effects). For example, 'Should nurses wear white uniforms?' might become 'What consequences does the wearing of white uniforms have (for example) on nurse–doctor–patient relationships, or on patients' attitudes?'.

9 See *Introduction to Social Research* (Punch, 1988), pp. 19–23.

10 See *Introduction to Social Research* (Punch, 1988), pp. 39–42.

4

Some Issues

CONTENTS

The last chapter dealt with an overall framework for developing proposals, and, as a practical and pedagogical device, focused on the central role of research questions. In this chapter, I look at the five issues listed above. Two of them (4.1 perspectives and 4.2 theory) concern the overall direction and orientation of the research; two of them (4.3 pre-structured–unfolding and 4.5 quantitative–qualitative) concern mostly design and methods; the other (4.4 the literature) is concerned both with the context of the research and with the way its research questions and strategy are developed.

These issues have particular prominence here because we are looking at quantitative and qualitative research together, and we are using the same general framework of research questions, design, data collection and data analysis to do that. They also come into focus because we are looking across social science research in general, including different areas and different research styles and traditions, as well as the two main different approaches. But the issues apply unevenly and in different ways across that range. Therefore not all will need explicit treatment in all proposals. Despite that, I think they are issues that should be routinely thought about, in planning research. Doing so will expose hidden assumptions, strengthen the proposal, and prepare the researcher better, especially if defence of the proposal (or, ultimately, of the dissertation) is involved.

In planning research and developing proposals, I think of these as issues that occur around and alongside the central 'what', 'how' and 'why' questions of the last chapter. In that sense, they give important context and direction to the proposed research. In some respects, too, they may change the way the 'what' questions are asked and dealt with.

The main point I want to stress here is that the writer needs to put the reader in the picture as to which of these points apply in the proposed research, and in what way. That means, of course, that the writer has to figure out in the planning stage of the research which of these points apply, and in what way. Doing this and communicating this is an important clarifying task for the researcher, and an important safeguard against mistaken expectations on the part of the reader.

4.1 THE PERSPECTIVE BEHIND THE RESEARCH

The issue here is whether there is a particular perspective, or philosophical position, or paradigm or metatheory, which lies behind and informs the research. The terms 'paradigm' and 'metatheory' now require a brief comment.

Paradigm here means a set of assumptions about the social world, and about what constitute proper techniques and topics for inquiring into that world. Put simply, it is a way of looking at the world. It means a view of how science should be done, and is a broad term encompassing elements of epistemology, theory and philosophy, along with methods.[1] Examples of general paradigms within social research are positivism, post-positivism, critical theory and constructivism. More detailed examples and classifications of paradigms are given by Guba and Lincoln (1994).

Some writers use the term *metatheory* similarly, to describe ideas about conceptions of science: 'Different thinkers, especially philosophers (of science) have suggested different ideas of what a scientist should and can do. Such thoughts about what is scientifically possible and what is not, are called metatheories' (Higgs, 1995: 3). Examples of metatheories considered by writers in the philosophy of education are logical empiricism (and post-empiricism), critical rationalism, critical theory, phenomenology, hermeneutics and systems theory.

The paradigms and metatheories noted above can also be thought of as 'perspectives' (or 'positions') which might lie behind a piece of social research. I will use the broader, more general (and less formidable!) term *perspective* here, to describe the idea that there might be a particular paradigm or metatheory or philosophical position behind the research. There are still other perspectives than those noted as paradigms and metatheories above which might apply in a piece of research, especially if it is qualitative. Examples are feminism, postmodernism, symbolic inter-actionism, semiotics, ethnomethodology, discourse analysis and conver-sation analysis.[2]

Adopting a particular perspective in a piece of research might influ-ence the researcher in several ways. For example, it usually means making certain assumptions and adopting certain systems of meaning, and reject-ing others. It might influence the researcher to focus on certain issues and to raise certain questions and problems for research. It might influence both the discourse and methods of the research – for example, favouring the use of certain methods, and 'prohibiting' certain others. It might influ-ence the way research questions are asked, with subsequent implications for methods, and there is also the point that different perspectives often imply different sets of criteria for evaluating a piece of social research (see, for example, Denzin and Lincoln, 1994: 479–83).

This issue of perspective, perhaps more than any other, applies unevenly across different social science areas, and its role and importance may be interpreted differently in different areas. Thus, it is more import-ant in some areas than others, and, especially in some applied social research contexts, it is not seen as relevant at all. It may also be applied differently at different levels of higher degree work – for example, it is often seen as a more appropriate concern at doctoral level than at masters level. Again, some areas of social research are heterogeneous and plural-istic when it comes to perspectives and paradigms, whereas others are relatively homogeneous. And finally, of course, and partly as a result of these points, some areas are more subject to paradigm disputes and debates than are others. Thus, educational research is both a hetero-geneous and a contested area on these issues, whereas experimental psy-chology is homogeneous and relatively free of such debates.

An implication of this is that it is hard to write on this issue in a way that would apply to all social research areas. Despite this, I would suggest three straightforward points that can assist students in developing their proposals.

First, I do not believe that all social research *has* to begin or proceed from one of these perspectives. On the contrary, research may proceed from the more 'pragmatic' approach of questions that need answers, or problems that need solutions. That was the position taken in *Introduction to Social Research* (Punch, 1988), a book concerned with introducing students to both the quantitative and the qualitative approaches in social research.

Second, and equally, a piece of social research *may well* proceed from some particular perspective, perhaps one of those mentioned above, or perhaps some combination of them. Examples would be a feminist study of participation in unions, a critical theory study of life in asylums, a constructivist study of curriculum development in science, and a post-positivist study of quality assurance procedures in education.

Third, if the second point applies, the proposal writer should identify that perspective early and clearly in the proposal. This is important in the interests of avoiding mistaken expectations on the part of readers.[3]

4.2 THE ROLE OF THEORY

The previous section used the term 'metatheory' to refer to a particular paradigm or perspective which might inform a piece of research. This present section is about what we might call 'substantive theory' and the role it plays in the research. By substantive theory I mean a theory about a substantive issue or phenomenon, some examples of which are shown below. Usually, the function of such a theory is both to describe and explain – an explanatory theory is one which not only describes but also explains the phenomenon of substantive interest. Thus, theory, in this sense, is a set of propositions which together describe and explain the phenomenon being studied. These propositions are at a higher level of abstraction than the specific facts and empirical generalizations (the data) about the phenomenon. They explain the data by deduction, in the if–then sense (see Section 4.2.2).

Like metatheory, this question about the role of substantive theory is sometimes considered more appropriate at the doctoral level than at the masters level. This seems to be because a common criterion among universities for the award of the doctorate centres on the 'substantial and original contribution to knowledge' the study makes, and the 'substantial' part of that criterion is often interpreted in terms of substantive theory.

Some examples of substantive theories from different areas of social research are attribution theory, reinforcement theory, various learning theories and personal construct theory (from psychology); reference group theory and social stratification theory (from sociology); the theory of vocational personalities and career anchors (from occupational sociology); theories of children's moral development and of teacher career cycles (from education) and various leadership theories (from management and administration).

Thus, the general question here, for the research proposal, is 'What is the role of (substantive) theory in this study?'. We can look at this question under two subsidiary questions:

- does the description–explanation distinction apply in the proposed project?
- does the theory-generation–theory-verification distinction apply?

4.2.1 Description versus explanation

Does the description–explanation distinction apply in the proposed study? This is one of those issues which does not necessarily apply to all studies, but is nonetheless a useful question to consider when designing the proposal.

Research, whether quantitative or qualitative, can be descriptive, or explanatory, or both. A *descriptive study* sets out to collect, organize and summarize information about the matter being studied. To describe is to draw a picture of what happened, or of how things are proceeding, or of what a situation or person or event is (or was) like, or means, or of how things are related to each other. It is concerned with making complicated things understandable. In social science, it often involves summarizing specific factual information into empirical generalizations (if the research has a nomothetic or generalizing bias), or summarizing details of events, characteristics, cases or processes (if the research has an idiographic or particularizing bias).

An *explanatory study*, on the other hand, sets out to explain and account for the descriptive information. It too is concerned with making complicated things understandable, but on a different level. It aims to find the reasons for things, showing why and how they are what they are.

Description is a more restricted purpose than explanation. We can describe without explaining, but we can't really explain without describing. Therefore explanation goes further than description – it is description plus something else. Broadly speaking, an explanatory study will be concerned with testing or verifying theory, or with generating theory, or with both of these.

One way to see the difference between description and explanation is to compare 'what-questions' with 'why- or how-questions'. A descriptive study asks, basically: 'What is the case or situation here?' An explanatory study asks, basically: 'Why is this the case or situation?' or 'How does (or did) this situation come about?'. This description–explanation distinction applies to both quantitative and qualitative studies. For qualitative research, Maxwell (1996: 59) has a third category of questions – interpretive questions. Thus descriptive questions ask 'What?', explanatory questions ask 'Why?' and interpretive questions ask about the meanings of things for the people involved.[4]

In my opinion, both descriptive and explanatory studies have their place in research, and one is not necessarily better than the other. Rather, it is a question of assessing the particular research area or situation, and especially of assessing what stage the development of knowledge in that area has reached, and designing the emphasis of the study accordingly. Thus, for a totally new research area (for example, how teachers use the internet in classrooms), it makes sense for research to have a descriptive emphasis. For a well-worked research area (for example, the relationship between social class and scholastic achievement), where considerable descriptive information already exists, it makes sense for research to have an explanatory emphasis.[5]

In some quarters, however, the value of a purely descriptive study might be questioned. There may well be a view, especially at the doctoral level, that a study should try to do more than 'just describe'. There is a good reason for this: explanatory knowledge is more powerful than descriptive knowledge. When we know why (or how) something happens, we know more than just what happens, and we can use the explanation for prediction. But, as a counter to that, and in addition to the example of a new research area given above, a very valuable step towards explanation can often be a careful and thorough description. A good first step in explaining why something happens is to describe exactly what happens. And careful descriptive work can be of great assistance in the development of more abstract concepts important in later theorizing. Also, some areas or styles of research have a different view on the merits of a descriptive study. An example is ethnography in anthropology (and in some applied social research areas), where 'full ethnographic description' may be the goal of the research.[6] Another is Glaser's view of the Strauss and Corbin approach in grounded theory – that it is not true grounded theory, but rather 'full conceptual description' (see especially Glaser, 1992).

Explanation itself is a complex philosophical concept. The view of explanation I am using here emphasizes induction from specific facts or empirical generalizations to more general and abstract propositions. The empirical generalization is then a specific example of the more general proposition, which thereby 'explains' it. Another frequent and useful, but different, form of explanation, is the 'missing links' form. Here, an event or empirical generalization is explained by showing the links which bring it about. Thus the relationship between social class and scholastic achievement might be explained by using cultural capital (Bourdieu, 1973) as the link between them. Or the relationship between social class and self esteem might be explained by using parent–child relationship as the link between them (Rosenberg, 1968: 54–82).[7]

To summarize, the questions for proposal development are:

- Is the proposed study descriptive, explanatory or both? In other words, does it aim to answer questions about 'what', or also about 'why' and 'how'?
- What is the logic behind the position taken, and how does that logic flow through the proposal?

4.2.2 Theory verification versus theory generation[8]

This is another issue which may apply unevenly across different social science areas. It is linked to the previous section through the concepts of explanation and explanatory theory. Broadly speaking, the two main possible roles for substantive explanatory theory in a study are testing theory or generating theory. The first is usually called theory verification, the second is theory generation. This theory verification–generation distinction cuts across the quantitative–qualitative distinction. A theory verification study can be quantitative or qualitative or both; so can a theory generation study. Either can be appropriate, depending on the research area, topic or context. Neither is better than the other. At the same time, it is historically true that theory verification studies in social science research have more often been quantitative, and theory generation studies have more often been qualitative.[9]

Once again, I am using theory here in the sense of substantive explanatory theory. In this sense, a theory is a set of statements which explains facts (observations, findings, or empirical generalizations). It is at a more abstract level than the facts themselves. There is an if–then connection between the theory and the facts: if the theory is true, then the factual statements follow. These factual statements are hypotheses to be tested in a theory verification study.

A theory verification study aims to test a theory or, more accurately, to test propositions (that is, hypotheses) derived from the theory. This is a very common model in social science areas which have traditionally emphasized quantitative research (such as psychology and some areas of education). Such a study starts with a theory, deduces hypotheses from it, and proceeds to test these hypotheses.

A theory generation study aims to generate or develop a theory to explain empirical phenomena or findings. Such a study typically starts with questions, moves to data and ends with a theory. This has been a common model in some qualitative research, especially where grounded theory is favoured (for example, nursing research).

This theory verification–generation distinction is really a matter of emphasis in a study. A theory verification study often ends up in theory modification or generation, especially if hypotheses are not confirmed. Similarly, a theory generation study will naturally use the processes of verification (and falsification) in constructing the theory. But, while the two may naturally get intertwined in doing the research, it is a good idea for a study to be clear at the proposal stage on which of the two is its main focus and objective.

A theory verification study has hypotheses for testing. Hypotheses are specific predictions about what is expected to be found in the data, paralleling research questions, and they should follow from (and be explained by) the theory. As noted earlier (Section 3.7.3), I see little point in having hypotheses without also showing the theory from which they follow.

Therefore the questions at proposal development stage are:

- If the purpose is explanatory, does the study focus on theory verification or theory generation?
- What is the logic behind this position and how does that logic flow through the proposal?
- If theory verification is the focus, what are the hypotheses and what is the theory behind them?

4.3 PRE-STRUCTURED VERSUS UNFOLDING[10]

This issue is about the amount of structure and specificity which is planned into the research, especially in its research questions, its conceptual framework and design, and its data. As noted earlier (Section 2.4), it is about the timing of such structure. Across the whole field of empirical social science research, studies may vary from tightly pre-planned and pre-structured to almost totally unfolding, with many positions between. This is therefore a central issue to be clear about in planning the research, and in communicating that plan through the proposal. The distinction applies especially to the research questions, the design and the data, and it may also include the conceptual framework.

As noted in Section 2.4, some types of research are highly pre-structured, with clear and specific research questions, a clear conceptual framework, a pre-planned design and pre-coded data. Some types of research, on the other hand, are not at all pre-structured. Specific research questions are not clear in advance, a general approach is described rather than a tightly pre-figured design, and data are not pre-structured. These things will emerge or unfold as the study progresses.

Figure 4.1 shows that these two descriptions represent the ends of a continuum, with varying degrees of pre-structuring or unfolding along the continuum.

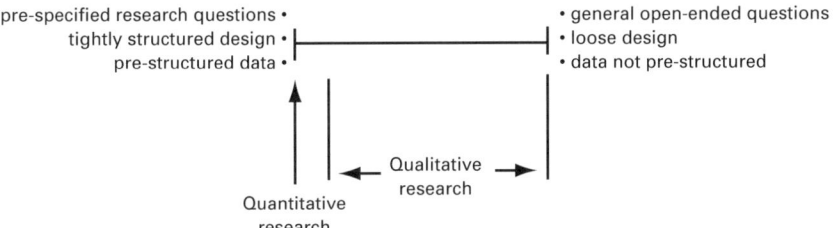

FIGURE 4.1   *Pre-specified versus unfolding: the timing of structure*

Once again, the point is not that one type is better than the other. Both have their place and both have their strengths and weaknesses. Rather than wanting to privilege one over the other, it is better that we think of adopting the type of research which is most appropriate for the area, topic and purposes of a particular project.

For the proposal, it is likely that projects towards the left hand end of this continuum will be easier to describe, lending themselves more to a formula-like approach to proposal development. Towards the right hand end, the proposal writer has a different problem, because there is no detailed research plan with a specific set of steps. Here, however, I think the proposal should indicate:

- that the study (or some part of it) is of the unfolding, emerging type;
- why this is appropriate for the area, topic and approach;
- in general terms, how structure and specificity will emerge during the research – how research questions will be identified, how the design will be developed and how the analysis will uncover structure in the data.

In other words, an unfolding type of study does not imply an 'anything goes' sort of proposal. Consider, for example, this statement from Eisner (1991: 241–2), writing about qualitative proposals in educational research:

> Lest these comments be interpreted by some to mean that no planning is necessary in conducting qualitative research, or that 'anything goes,' as they say, I want to make it clear that this is not how my words should be interpreted. Planning is necessary. Nevertheless, it should not and cannot function as a recipe or as a script. Evidence matters. One has a responsibility to support what one says, but support does not require measured evidence. Coherence, plausibility, and utility are quite acceptable in trying to deal with social complexity. My point is not to advocate anarchy or to reduce the study of schools and classrooms to a Rorschach projection, it is to urge that the analysis of a research proposal or a research study should employ criteria appropriate to the genre. Professors who make such assessments should understand, as should graduate students, the nature of the genre, what constitutes appropriate criteria, and why they are appropriate.

We return to this question in Section 6.3.

4.4 THE RELEVANT LITERATURE[11]

All social research has a relevant literature, and no research takes place in a vacuum. It is part of the researcher's responsibility to identify the literature which is relevant to the study, to be familiar with it, to locate the present study in relation to the literature, and to determine how the literature will be handled in both the proposal and in the study.

I believe there is no one right way to deal with the relevant literature in a study. Rather, there are various possible ways, some of which are indicated below. The researcher's job is to determine the position taken with respect to the literature, and to articulate that position in the proposal.

The literature is an extremely valuable resource, and an important storehouse of knowledge and thinking about a topic or area. It includes previous research reports and their findings, theorizing and reflections about the topic or area, literature reviews in the area and any other documentary material. While acknowledging the value of the literature as a storehouse of knowledge, it is important also for the researcher to take a critical stance towards that literature, especially in assessing previous research. 'Critical' in this sense does not only mean applying criticism, though that certainly can occur. It also means taking an analytical approach in dealing with the literature (Brink and Wood, 1994: 58), and critically reflecting on its organization, completeness, coherence and consistency.

For proposal development, I suggest three guiding questions about the relevant literature, as follows.

(a) *What literature is relevant to this project?* It is necessary first to identify what body of literature is relevant to the proposed study and to indicate awareness of it. How the literature will be dealt with is discussed in (b) and (c) below.

Some points to remember about identifying the relevant literature are the following.

- Different research areas and topics will have different quantities of relevant literature. In some areas the volume of literature will be vast, in some areas relatively small.
- More than one body of literature might be relevant (for example, theoretical literature vs research literature and findings; or the proposed topic might cut across more than one substantive area).
- The literature will vary in its degree of relevance to your study – some will be centrally relevant, some only peripherally relevant.
- Once again, the levels-of-abstraction issue arises. Be careful of saying 'there is no relevant literature for my topic'. This statement may be true at a specific level, but not true at a more abstract level.[12]
- As well as traditional literature-searching methods, the internet today is a valuable resource for locating relevant literature.

(b) *What is the relationship of the proposed study to its relevant literature?* This includes such questions as: Where does the proposed study fit in relation to its relevant literature? What is its connection to that literature? How will the proposed research move beyond previous work or beyond what we already know?

There are several possible answers to these questions. For example, the proposed research may fill a gap in the literature; it may sit in line with the main trends in the literature, seeking to extend those; it may take a quite different direction from those in the literature; it may aim to confirm, challenge or disconfirm other findings, as in a replication study; it may test or extend a theory from the literature, or it may use a theoretical framework or model from the literature. There are other possibilities as well, so the general question to be dealt with in the proposal is 'What contribution will this study make to the literature?'.

(c) *How will the proposed study deal with the literature and how will the argument in the proposal use the literature?* There are different ways a study may deal with its literature, and different expectations that may be held for the use of the literature in the proposal. The following are examples.

- The literature may be fully reviewed in advance of the research; the full literature review is part of the proposal and is included or attached.
- The literature may be reviewed, but the review has not been done at proposal submission time; in this case, part of the review, a sample of the review, or themes to be used in the review, may be included with the proposal.
- The literature will be reviewed, analysed and incorporated as the study progresses, and perhaps especially when the study's data are being analysed and its findings are being discussed. An example of this is a grounded theory study. When this approach to the literature is proposed, it is worth giving a clear statement of and justification for it, if only because of expectations sometimes held that the literature will be reviewed ahead of the research.

As to how the proposal itself uses the literature, I think good advice on this matter is provided by Locke et al. (1993: 71–2), when they write that the proposal writer should place the research question(s) – or hypotheses – in the context of previous work in such a way as to explain and justify the decisions made for the proposed study, especially with respect to (a) how and why the research question or hypothesis was formulated in the present form, and (b) why the proposed research strategy was selected. They see no other role for the literature *in the research proposal*, and regard the heading 'review of the literature' as inappropriate in a proposal. Similar advice comes from Maxwell (1996). Clearly, this has the benefit of shortening the proposal. On the other hand, the student needs to check departmental expectations on this question.

Whatever position you take on the literature, remember that, at higher degree level, you will be expected to be familiar with the relevant literature in your area. Remember also that good literature reviews are extremely valuable, tying a field together and showing us the state of knowledge in an area, its trends and its gaps. They show us 'where things are up to' in that area, what we already know and, just as important, what is contested and what we don't know. They are also difficult and time consuming to do. Therefore, if you find a good literature review, it is sensible to use it, of course with appropriate acknowledgements.[13]

Two common criticisms of literature reviews in dissertations are that they are not thematic, and that they are not properly integrated with the study. While your proposal may not contain a full literature review, it is worth bearing these criticisms in mind during proposal development, knowing that the dissertation itself will need a literature review. Both criticisms can be addressed by developing an organizing framework for dealing with the literature, as it is located and read. This is part of reading critically and analytically, and the organizing framework you develop will often be the basis of your study's conceptual framework. It will help to make your ultimate literature review both thematic – rather than merely a serialized or chronological summary of what others have done – and integrated with your study. The present study needs to be connected to that literature, so that there is some point to the literature review. It is best to avoid unintegrated chronological summaries – a literature review is not the same as an annotated bibliography.

Finally, in some research areas, your literature review will need to be selective. For some topics, the volume of related literature is so great that a dissertation literature review cannot be comprehensive, covering everything.[14] In these cases, the researcher is forced to be selective. When that occurs, the writer should indicate why it is being done, and the basis on which the selection is made. Here is where previous reviews of the literature, if available and relatively contemporary, can be extremely valuable. It is worth remembering that completed dissertations normally contain a literature review. Finding a recent dissertation on (or close to) your topic can save you a lot of time and work. Remember your departmental dissertation library, Dissertation Abstracts International, and other sources of dissertation abstracts.

4.5 QUANTITATIVE, QUALITATIVE OR BOTH?[15]

Obviously, this is a fundamental issue of approach and method. As noted earlier, a full consideration of the quantitative–qualitative distinction would cover approaches to conceptualizing social reality, as well as design, methods and data. At the practical level, the distinction comes down most often to data and methods. The framework behind *Introduction to Social Research* (Punch, 1988), and which I have found to be most useful in teaching students, works backwards from the nature of the data. In that framework, the data which empirical research requires can be quantitative, qualitative, or both. Quantitative data (numbers) are produced by quantitative methods, and qualitative data (mostly words) are produced by qualitative methods.

Thus, any proposal needs to be very clear on the extent to which the research will:

- use quantitative methods and data;
- use qualitative methods and data;
- combine the two types of methods and data.

If it combines the two approaches, it should be clear on which research questions involve quantitative methods and data, and which involve qualitative methods and data, and which involve both. It should also be clear on the sort of combination that will be involved, given the various different models as to how this can be done.

On this question (quantitative, qualitative, or both?), perhaps more than any other issue, the proposal should demonstrate internal validity. Here, that means that its methods should match its questions, and its argument should be clear and internally consistent. In line with the passing of the 'paradigm wars' and of the associated quantitative–qualitative debate, there is an increasing tendency in a number of social science areas to combine the two approaches, bringing the two types of methods and data together.

4.6 REVIEW CONCEPTS AND QUESTIONS

> *Concepts*
>
> paradigm
> metatheory
> perspective
> substantive theory
> descriptive study
> explanatory study
> theory verification
> theory generation
> hypotheses – relationship to theory
> pre-structured study
> unfolding study
> relevant literature
> quantitative data (and methods)
> qualitative data (and methods)
> internal validity

Questions

- Perspective

  Is there a particular perspective (or paradigm, or metatheory) behind the research?

- (Substantive) theory

  What is the role of theory in my study?

  - Does the description–explanation distinction apply? Is my study descriptive, explanatory or both? What is the logic behind my position?
  - Does the theory-generation–theory-verification distinction apply? If my purpose is explanatory, is the focus on generation or verification of theory? What is the logic behind my position?
  - If my focus is theory verification, what are the hypotheses and what is the theory behind them?

- Pre-structured versus unfolding

  To what extent is my study pre-structured or unfolding? Does this apply differentially to different parts of my study?

- Relevant literature

  What literature is relevant to my study?
  What is the relationship of my study to this literature?
  How will my study deal with the literature, and how does my proposal use the literature?

- Methods and data

  Does my study use quantitative methods and data, qualitative methods and data, or both?

NOTES

1 Guba and Lincoln (1994: 107) write as follows: 'A paradigm may be viewed as a set of *basic beliefs* (or metaphysics) that deals with ultimates or first principles. It represents a *worldview* that defines, for its holder, the nature of "the world", the individual's place in it, and the range of possible relationships to that world and its parts, as, for example, cosmologies and theologies do.'

2 There is some confusion and overlap of terms here – for example, it becomes difficult to separate paradigm–metatheory–perspective from strategy, and strategy from design. Thus Morse (1994: 224–5) sees semiotics as a paradigm, ethnomethodology and discourse analysis as strategies, and phenomenology as both paradigm and strategy. She also (p. 221) writes about 'paradigmatic perspectives'. One way to minimize this difficulty of demarcation is to use perspective as a broad term (including paradigm and metatheory), to see strategy as something which implements a perspective, and design as something which implements a strategy. Appendix 1 elaborates this use of perspective, strategy and design.

3 I realize that the issue of perspective (or paradigm) is always present even if implicitly, including in 'pragmatic' research, since assumptions about reality and strategies and methods of inquiry are always involved. I know too that a case can be made for insisting on the articulation of these assumptions in research proposals. But I have found that a strong emphasis on perspectives and paradigm issues can leave *beginning* research students confused, and bogged down. In my teaching, therefore, I now prefer most of the time to 'back into' the issue of perspective, letting it emerge as appropriate rather than insisting on or forcing its emergence. The question of the defence of that perspective, if any is required, is a matter that appears to be department-specific (or perhaps university-specific). One department might insist on a detailed articulation and defence of the perspective adopted, whereas another might not. In view of this, it is good advice for the student to see 'how the land lies' on this issue in the department in question.

4 More completely, Maxwell (1996: 59–60) defines five categories of understanding in qualitative research – description, interpretation, theory (explanation), generalization and evaluation. The first three categories include most types of questions that qualitative researchers develop.

5 A classic example of this is Durkheim's (1951) work on suicide. He assembled existing descriptive information (in the form of empirical generalizations) and theorized 'upwards' from them to an explanation.

6 This is not to imply that all ethnographic research has the goal of description.

7 These are examples from quantitative research, where the concept of intervening variables is used to describe the links. In Maxwell's (1996: 58) terms, this type of explanation is variance theory explanation. But the logic works just as well with qualitative data (see Miles and Huberman, 1994: 222–8). In this case, it is termed process theory explanation.

8 See *Introduction to Social Research* (Punch, 1998), pp. 14–19, 166–7.

9 Creswell (1994: 81–101) has a particularly useful discussion on the role of theory, showing its typical deductive structure for theory testing quantitative research, and its typical inductive structure for theory generating qualitative research.

10 See *Introduction to Social Research* (Punch, 1988), pp. 23–7.

11 See *Introduction to Social Research* (Punch, 1988), pp. 43–4, 167–8.

12 For example, there may well be no literature or previous research on, say, the educational performance of aboriginal children in Narrogin, Western Australia. But aboriginal children are an indigenous ethnic minority; Narrogin is a rural community. Now the relevant literature is broader: the educational performance of indigenous ethnic minorities in rural communities.

13 A recent book by Hart (1998) provides a comprehensive treatment of the task of reviewing literature for a Masters or doctoral dissertation. In addition, many books contain a section or chapter on locating and reviewing the relevant literature: examples are Bell (1993: 33–51), Borg and Gall (1989: 114–66) and Delamont et al. (1997: 51–66). Creswell (1994: 20–40) has a chapter on the use of the literature in both quantitative and qualitative research. A specialized technique for reviewing and synthesizing research findings in an area is meta-analysis (Rosenthal, 1991).

14 Examples of such areas would be the literature on change and innovations in organizations, or on personality theory, or on leadership research.

15 See *Introduction to Social Research* (Punch, 1988), pp. 4–5, 57–62, 239–50.

Methods

5.1 INTRODUCTION

For ease of presentation of the material in this chapter, I will assume at this point in the research planning process that we now have a stable set of specific research questions, connected with each other, integrated with general research questions and forming a coherent whole, and satisfying the empirical criterion. The proposal can now deal with the methods for the research. In other words, since we now know what data will be needed (design), we can focus on how to get the data (data collection), and on what to do with the data once collected (data analysis).

This chapter does not cover research methods in detail. *Introduction to Social Research* (Punch, 1998), together with the associated reading indicated there, does that, in Chapters 5, 6 and 7 for quantitative research, and Chapters 8, 9 and 10 for qualitative research. Rather, I deal now in general terms with the three main issues any piece of research must deal with, once it has settled on its research questions – *design, data collection* and *data analysis*. Since *sampling* is implicated in all three of these issues, but especially in design and data collection, I will discuss that in general terms also. The guiding question throughout this chapter is: *What needs to be said about each of these matters in the proposal?* Each section in the chapter therefore makes suggestions about that.

Before looking at these topics in the light of that question, I look again at the overriding question of quantitative data, qualitative data, or both, and end the chapter by looking at the general question of methodological expertise.

5.2 QUANTITATIVE DATA, QUALITATIVE DATA, OR BOTH?[1]

Sometimes the logic of a study, including the way research questions (or hypotheses) are framed, is clearly quantitative or clearly qualitative, and that logic flows through naturally into the design, sampling, data collection and data analysis.

As a quantitative example, perhaps the conceptualization of the problem and questions in the proposal is in terms of an experimental comparison, based on some intervention or treatment, with clear outcome variables in mind. This clearly involves quantitative methods and data. As a qualitative example, perhaps the research has been conceptualized as an ethnographic case study, focusing on interpretations, meanings and the cultural significance of some behaviour. Equally clearly, this involves qualitative data. Or, as a mixed-methods example, perhaps a quantitative survey is to be followed by qualitative interviewing.

Quite often, however, the student researcher can get to the point of having research questions, and of now having to confront methodological issues, without clear implications from what has gone before about whether the data should be quantitative or qualitative. In other words, the research could be done either way. Hence the question arises: quantitative data (and methods), qualitative data (and methods), or both? Six suggestions for dealing with this choice are discussed in some detail in *Introduction to Social Research* (Punch, 1988). In summary form they are as follows.

- Re-examine the research questions and the way they are phrased – what implications for data are there?
- Are we interested in making standardized comparisons, sketching contours and dimensions, quantifying relationships between variables and accounting for variance? Or are we more interested in studying a phenomenon or situation in detail, holistically and in context, focusing on interpretations and/or processes?
- What guidance do we find from the literature about this topic on this methodological question?
- What are the practical consequences of each alternative (including resources)?
- Which way would we learn more?
- Which sort of research is more 'my style'?

Very often, the question focuses entirely on the data themselves, in which case it really becomes: to measure or not to measure? This is because measurement is the process of turning data into numbers, and is therefore the operation which differentiates quantitative data from qualitative data.

Often, too, this matter is the subject of some misconceptions, where students feel they must (or must not) develop or use measuring instruments. I strongly prefer a commonsense answer to the question 'to measure or not to measure', based on an understanding of what measurement is, and of how it can help us in answering research questions and in building knowledge. When looked at this way, I think there are many 'ambiguous'[2] empirical research situations where measurement helps.

Dealing with this commonly occurring and often perplexing question (quantitative or qualitative data? or, to measure or not to measure?) is often made easier by remembering these four practical points: (a) get the research questions clear; (b) as far as possible, let questions dictate the nature of the data; (c) measure if it is feasible and helpful to do so,[3] and (d) use both types of data, if appropriate.

5.3 DESIGN[4]

I focus here on a view of the term 'research design' general enough to accommodate both quantitative and qualitative approaches. This general idea of design is one of situating the researcher in the empirical world. On a practical level, it means connecting the research questions to data. Design sits between the research questions and the data, showing how the research questions will be connected to the data, and what tools and procedures to use in answering them. Therefore it needs to follow from the questions, and to fit in with the data.

The design is the basic plan for a piece of empirical research,[5] and includes four main ideas: strategy, conceptual framework, who or what will be studied, and the tools and procedures to be used for collecting and analysing empirical materials. Thus there are four main questions for research design. The data will be collected and analysed:

- following what strategy?
- within what framework?
- from whom?
- how?

These questions overlap, especially the first two. Also the second question, in particular, is more typical of quantitative designs, although it does apply in some qualitative research. We will now look briefly at each of the four questions.

5.3.1 Strategy

Following what strategy? At the centre of the design of a study is its internal logic or rationale – the reasoning, or the set of ideas, by which the study intends to proceed in order to answer its research questions. The term 'strategy' refers to that. Thus, in quantitative research, the experiment includes a strategy, designed to achieve certain comparisons. So does the correlational survey, though it is conceptualized and designed differently. Similarly, in qualitative research, a multiple case study involves a strategy for setting up certain comparisons. Ethnography and grounded theory are strategies the qualitative researcher might use, and ethnomethodology, discourse analysis and life history are others. Answers to the question 'Following what strategy?' will thus differ according to whether the approach is quantitative or qualitative. Associated with this question of strategy is another important question: to what extent will the researcher manipulate or organize the research situation, as against studying it naturalistically? In other words, to what extent will the researcher intervene in the research situation, contriving it and constructing it for research purposes, as against studying it as it occurs naturally? Quantitative research design can vary from extremely interventionist to non-interventionist. Qualitative research design is generally non-interventionist.

Therefore, what needs to be said about the strategy in a proposal depends on whether a quantitative or qualitative study is proposed.

- If the study is quantitative, which quantitative strategy is proposed?
- If qualitative, which qualitative strategy is proposed?
- If there is a combination of quantitative and qualitative approaches, what is the proposed mixture of strategies?

Some of the most commonly used strategies are the experiment, the quasi-experiment and the correlational survey for quantitative research, and case studies, ethnography and grounded theory for qualitative research. Appendix 1 gives more complete lists of quantitative and qualitative research strategies.

Whether quantitative or qualitative, the researcher needs to describe the planned strategy procedurally, as well as generically. 'Generically' means identifying the strategy in general terms – for example, case study, ethnography, survey or quasi-experiment. That description is necessary, but only part of what is required. 'Procedurally' means saying how the researcher will execute the general strategy. To quote from Dreher (1994: 289):

> In general, terms such as *ethnography, participant observation, grounded theory,* and *fieldwork* are not useful to a reviewer unless they are described procedurally, in relation to the specific proposal. For example, participant observation

is perhaps the most pervasive technique used in ethnographic designs, yet we know that the investigator cannot participate and observe everywhere at the same time. Methodological choices must be made about where and when observations take place. Although some of these decisions necessarily are made in the actual process of the research, from the emerging data, the investigator should be able to provide reviewers with a general outline of observations that is consistent with the problem being researched.

The point being made here in a qualitative context applies just as well to quantitative research strategies and designs.

5.3.2 Framework[6]

Within what framework? Framework here means conceptual framework – the conceptual status of the things being studied, and their relationship to each other. Pre-specified research questions are often accompanied by a clear conceptual framework, and developing and describing that framework can help in clarifying the research questions. The structure continuum (Figure 4.1) applies to the conceptual framework as well – it may be developed ahead of the study, or it may emerge as the study progresses. Quantitative designs typically have well-developed pre-specified frameworks, whereas qualitative designs show much more variability, from clear pre-specified frameworks, to 'first approximations', to no pre-specified framework at all.

For the proposal, therefore:

- if your study has a pre-determined conceptual framework, the proposal should show it; this can often be done effectively using a diagram;
- if this conceptual framework is seen as only an initial version or approximation, for modification as the study progresses, this should be noted in the proposal;
- if you have an unfolding study, where a conceptual framework will be developed during the research, this too should be noted and explained.

5.3.3 Sample[7]

From whom will the data be collected? This question concerns sampling for the research. In this form, the question is biased towards quantitative studies. The more general question *'Who or what will be studied?'* (Denzin and Lincoln, 1994) covers both quantitative and qualitative approaches.

All empirical research involves sampling – in the words of Miles and Huberman (1994: 27): 'You cannot study everyone everywhere doing everything'. The researcher thus needs to think through the sampling aspects of the study in preparing the proposal.

It is best if the sampling plan is seen as part of the internal logic of the study, rather than as an afterthought to be considered when data collection is close. This means it needs to fit into the study's logic, to follow from it and to be consistent with it. This is an overriding general principle about sampling, whatever type of research is involved. After that, it is difficult to suggest detailed rules about sampling, since the appropriate sampling plan for a study depends very much on what the study is trying to find out, and on its strategy for doing that.

Thus, for quantitative research, the sampling may be probabilistic (if representativeness is important) or purposive (if, for example, the point of the research is to study a relationship between variables). For qualitative research, many different sampling strategies are used. Table 5.1 shows some of the possibilities.

For the proposal, therefore, the researcher needs to see sampling as part of the planning process for the research, to select among sampling possibilities in line with the logic of the study, and to indicate the sampling plan in the proposal.

If the study is quantitative, the proposal should indicate:

- the sampling strategy, especially whether it is purposive, representative or both, and what claims will be made for the generalizability of findings;
- how big the sample will be;
- how it will be selected.

This description of the sampling plan should include justification of the sample size, since there are established methods for determining appropriate sample size in quantitative research. This is a technical matter, which essentially involves balancing cost and access against the level of precision required in relation to the variability of the population on the characteristics being measured. Also, the power of the statistical test to be used needs to be considered (Moser and Kalton, 1979; Lipsey, 1990) and many computer packages now include this (Schofield, 1996).

If the study is qualitative, the proposal should similarly indicate:

- the sampling strategy, including what intention (if any) there is for the generalizability of findings;
- the extent of the proposed sample;
- how sample units will be chosen.

Qualitative sample sizes tend to be small, with no statistical grounds for guidance. The sample size here is usually a function of the purpose of the study in the light of its sampling frames and of practical constraints.

TABLE 5.1   *Sampling strategies in qualitative inquiry*

Type of sampling	Purpose
Maximum variation	Documents diverse variations and identifies important common patterns
Homogeneous	Focuses, reduces, simplifies, facilitates group interviewing
Critical case	Permits logical generalization and maximum application of information to other cases
Theory based	Finding examples of a theoretical construct and thereby elaborating and examining it
Confirming and disconfirming cases	Elaborating initial analysis, seeking exceptions, looking for variation
Snowball or chain	Identifies cases of interest from people who know people who know what cases are information-rich
Extreme or deviant case	Learning from highly unusual manifestations of the phenomenon of interest
Typical case	Highlights what is normal or average
Intensity	Information-rich cases that manifest the phenomenon intensely, but not extremely
Politically important case	Attracts desired attention or avoids attracting undesired attention
Random purposeful	Adds credibility to sample when potential purposeful sample is too large
Stratified purposeful	Illustrates subgroups; facilitates comparisons
Criterion	All cases that meet some criterion; useful for quality assurance
Opportunistic	Following new leads; taking advantage of the unexpected
Combination or mixed	Triangulation, flexibility, meets multiple interests and needs
Convenience	Saves time, money and effort, but at the expense of information and credibility

Source: Miles and Huberman (1994: 28)

For some qualitative strategies too, there is no pre-determined sample size. An example is grounded theory, where theoretical sampling – successive sampling of data guided by the theoretical trends emerging from the analysis – guides the work. Such a strategy should be indicated.[8] If a case study is involved, the basis of case selection should be made clear, as should the basis of within-case sampling. If sampling of documentary or other qualitative material is proposed, its basis needs to be shown.

5.3.4 Data collection (instruments, procedures)

How will the data be collected? This question asks about the instruments and procedures to be used in data collection, topics dealt with in Chapters 6 and 7 of *Introduction to Social Research* (Punch, 1988) for quantitative research, and Chapters 9 and 10 for qualitative research. We need to differentiate this section according to whether the data are quantitative or qualitative. We get quantitative data from counting, scaling, or both. Qualitative data are most likely to be words, which we get by asking (interviewing), watching (observation) or reading (documents), or some combination of these three activities.[9]

Instruments – quantitative data[10]
Quantitative data collection instruments are questionnaires, standardized measuring instruments, ad hoc rating scales or observation schedules. Whichever of these is involved, this question often arises in planning research: will I use an existing measuring instrument, or will I develop instruments (in whole or in part) specifically for this study? Either choice, or some combination of the two, can be acceptable, depending on the particular study. Each alternative has implications for what is included in the proposal. Thus:

- if the decision is to use existing data collection instruments, a brief description of their history, use in research and their psychometric characteristics should be included;
- if the decision is to construct an instrument(s) specifically for this study, an outline of the steps involved in doing that should be given, showing what pre-testing is involved.[11]

Instruments – qualitative data[12]
The question of instruments for qualitative data collection is both more contentious, and more difficult to summarize. There is a range of possibilities here. At one end of the range, the idea of an 'instrument' to collect qualitative data, with its connotations of standardization and quantification, is quite inappropriate. Instead, in this sort of research, the researcher is seen as the primary instrument for data collection and analysis. Qualitative data are mediated through this human instrument, rather than through other instruments (Creswell, 1994: 145).[13]

At the other end of the range, qualitative data collection instruments may begin to resemble quantitative ones. Examples would be the questionnaire for a qualitative survey, where open-ended questions are involved, or the schedule for qualitative interviews, where standardization across respondents is involved. Here, the same questions arise as above, namely: do I use instruments already developed, or will I develop my own for this research? It is more likely that the qualitative researcher will develop instruments, rather than use those developed by others. But either way, similar considerations apply to the proposal. If others' instruments are to be used, their background and previous use should be sketched. If instruments are to be developed for this study, it is appropriate to indicate the steps to be followed in developing them.

Additional possibilities for data in qualitative studies include documents, diaries and journals, other written materials and non-written qualitative data such as audio-visual materials or artefacts.

Thus, the following apply for the proposal.

- A general plan for proposed qualitative fieldwork should be shown; if the researcher is the 'instrument' for data collection, it is appropriate for the proposal to indicate this;
- If interviews are involved, what type of interviews, and especially what degree of structure and standardization is proposed? If standardized interview schedules are to be used, how will they be developed and pre-tested?
- Similarly, if qualitative questionnaires are proposed, what will be the degree of structure and standardization? How would they be developed and (if appropriate) pre-tested?
- The same considerations apply for observational data – what degree of structure and standardization is proposed, and how would proposed schedules be developed and pre-tested?
- If documents are to be used, which ones and why? Are there sampling or access considerations?
- If diaries, journals, critical incident reports, or other qualitative materials are involved, how would the collection of these, including any sampling aspects, be organized?

Procedures[14]

Procedures refer to the actual process of data collection, over and above any instruments proposed. If instruments are involved, the question here is how the instruments will be used or administered? In other words, what will be the actual data collection procedures? If fieldwork is involved, how would it be carried out?

Some examples can indicate the sorts of issues involved.

- If tests or rating scales are to be used, how will they be administered (face to face? one-to-one or group administration? by mail? by telephone? via the internet?).
- If interviews are involved, where will the interviews be conducted (at the office? at home? somewhere else?). When will they be done (working hours? outside working hours?). How will the recording be done (by taking notes? by reconstruction after the interview? by tape recorder?).

- If observation is involved, will it be overt or covert? How will you do it? How will observational data be recorded?

While the proposal may not answer all procedural questions, it should nonetheless indicate an awareness of the procedural and methodological choices ahead in the research.

Ethical issues

Data collection procedures need to be organized both to maximize the quality of data, and to deal with the related issues of access and ethics.

Since researchers cannot demand access to people, situations or data for research purposes, assistance and permission are involved. These are necessarily linked to ethical issues. It is wise to include these questions of access and ethics in the research planning process.[15]

Following Miles and Huberman (1994: 290–7), if the overall integrity, quality and worthiness of the research are conveyed by the proposal itself, the main recurrent ethical issues to be considered, and the questions central to them are:

- informed consent – do the people I wish to study have full information about the research, including why and how they have been chosen to participate? Is their consent freely given? What about if children are involved?
- privacy – in what ways will the research intrude into people's privacy?
- confidentiality and anonymity – how will the information be safe-guarded and the identity of people or institutions protected? How will anonymity be preserved?
- ownership of data and conclusions – after collection and analysis who owns the data and the conclusions? How will the research results be reported and disseminated?
- use and misuse of results – do I have an obligation to help my find-ings be used appropriately, and not to be misused?

Less frequent, but still important, ethical issues involve:

- honesty and trust (what is my relationship with the people I am study-ing?)
- reciprocity (what do participants gain from my research?)
- intervention and advocacy (what do I do if I see or hear about harmful, illegal, or wrongful behaviour during my research?)
- harm and risk (what might this research do to hurt the people involved?)

Sometimes, submission of the proposal requires a completed ethics check-list, which may have a separate format. This is another instance where you should check practices, guidelines and requirements in your department and university.

Thus, for the proposal, data collection procedures raise three main questions:

- quality of data – how will the proposed data collection and recording procedures ensure that data of the best quality will be obtained?
- access – how will the researcher obtain access to the people, situations, and/or information required for the research?
- ethics – what ethical issues are involved in the proposed data collection procedures and how will they be handled?

5.3.5 Data analysis[16]

How will data be analysed? After design and data collection, the other main methodological question concerns what will be done with the data once they have been collected. What methods of analysis will be used?

Quantitative data analysis involves statistics. *Introduction to Social Research* (Punch, 1988: Ch. 7) lays out the logic of the main statistical techniques, and recommends multiple regression analysis as a generalized data analysis approach. Qualitative data analysis has been a rapidly developing field in the past 20 or so years, and there are now many different data analysis varieties and possibilities for research. *Introduction to Social Research* (Punch, 1988: Ch. 10) presents an overview of some of the main directions in qualitative data analysis, putting special emphasis on grounded theory as an analytic approach.

For the proposal, you should indicate, at least in general terms, what analytic techniques you propose to use, in order to analyse the data you will collect. The proposal should also indicate what computer programs (if any) will be used in the analysis, whatever the type of data. In my experience, data analysis is an area where students will often need to seek expert advice, because of the issue of methodological expertise.

5.4 THE QUESTION OF METHODOLOGICAL EXPERTISE

A recurrent question now arises, for both quantitative and qualitative approaches: how much methodological expertise should the student researcher be expected to show at the proposal stage? By 'methodological expertise', I mean expertise in the particular methods or techniques proposed. This question is probably most acute and most visible at the data analysis stage, but it can involve other areas as well (for example, sampling, measurement, interviewing skills). Here are two examples of it:

- A quantitative survey is proposed, focusing on the relationships between different variables (this is the correlational survey). The researcher, quite appropriately, proposes to use regression analysis as the main data analysis approach and technique. To what extent should we expect that the researcher should know the technical aspects of regression analysis at the proposal stage?
- A qualitative study is proposed, with the objective of generating a substantive theory of the phenomenon being studied. The researcher, again quite appropriately, proposes to use grounded theory as the main data analysis approach and technique. To what extent should we expect the researcher to know the technical aspects of grounded theory analysis at the proposal stage?

Here again, different universities and departments may have differing views on this matter. It is wise, therefore, to check relevant expectations with the department you are working in. My view on this now is different from the view I held (say) 20 years ago. Today (in contrast to then), I would not require the candidate to demonstrate methodological mastery of a technique at the proposal stage. If it can be demonstrated, well and good, but I believe it is unrealistic today to require it. However, as a minimum, I think it is reasonable at the proposal stage to require the candidate to:

- have thought about what is required for the data analysis stage of the work;
- have developed – perhaps with expert assistance – at least a general idea of what technique(s) would be required and how they would be applied;
- be able to show how that fits in with the overall logic of the study.

In other words, I think it is sufficient for the candidate's knowledge to be at a logical rather than technical level at the proposal stage. I think that translates into a statement such as as: 'I can see that I will need such-and-such a technique (for example, regression analysis, or grounded theory) to analyse my data, because it will answer my research questions by showing how these independent variables relate to the dependent variables (regression analysis) or by enabling me to identify abstract grounded core concepts around which a theory can be built (grounded theory)'. Such a statement can be made by a student who has not yet developed technical mastery of the data analysis method, but has a logical understanding of how it operates and where it can be used. Developing this logical level of understanding is important, and it is a significant part of the learning which should occur through proposal preparation.

In short, I think it is acceptable for the student not to have developed technical mastery at the proposal stage, ahead of the research. My reasoning is that the student will develop that mastery on the way through the research, and should be able to demonstrate it after completing the research. But having said that, it is surely all to the good, and to be encouraged, if the student can develop technical mastery ahead of the research.

5.5 REVIEW CONCEPTS AND QUESTIONS

Concepts

design
strategy
conceptual framework
sample, sampling plan
data collection instruments
data collection procedures
data analysis
access
ethical issues
quality of data

Questions

- Will my study use quantitative methods and data, qualitative methods and data, or both?

- What strategy(ies) will my study use?

  - If the study is quantitative, which quantitative strategy is proposed?
  - If qualitative, which qualitative strategy is proposed?
  - If there is a combination of quantitative and qualitative approaches, what is the proposed mixture of strategies?

- Does my study have a conceptual framework?

  - Can this be shown in a diagram?
  - Is this an initial version, for modification as the study progresses?
  - Will my study develop a conceptual framework?

- Who or what will be studied?

- From whom will data be collected? Whether quantitative or qualitative:
  - What is the sample plan?
  - How big will the sample be (and why)?
  - How will sample units be selected?

- How will I collect the data?
  - If existing instruments are to be used, what is known about them?
  - If data collection instruments are to be developed, what steps will be followed?
  - If qualitative fieldwork is involved, what is the data collection plan?
  - What data collection procedures will be used?

- How will these procedures ensure that data of the best quality will be obtained?
- How will I obtain consent and access to the people, situations and/or information required for the research?
- What ethical issues are involved in the proposed data collection procedures and how will they be handled?
- How will I analyse my data?
  - What computer packages (if any) are involved?

NOTES

1 See *Introduction to Social Research* (Punch, 1988), pp. 57–62, 90–3, 244–50.
2 'Ambiguous' in the sense that the research question(s) could be addressed using either quantitative or qualitative data.
3 The distinction between the measurement of 'major' variables using established instruments, and measurement using researcher-constructed, ad hoc rating scales, is useful here – see *Introduction to Social Research* (Punch, 1988), pp. 90–3.
4 See *Introduction to Social Research* (Punch, 1988), pp. 65–87, 138–72.
5 Brink and Wood (1994) use the term 'blueprint'; Denzin and Lincoln (1994: 200) use 'roadmap'.
6 See *Introduction to Social Research* (Punch, 1988), pp. 66–8, 149–50.
7 See *Introduction to Social Research* (Punch, 1988), pp. 66–8, 105–6, 193–5.
8 In my experience, however, it is still wise in such cases to anticipate questions about sample size.

9 In either approach, the proposal for the research may be to work (in whole or in part) with data which already exist. This is known as *secondary analysis* – the term used for the reanalysis of previously collected and analysed data. In such a case, the proposal should discuss instruments, procedures and sample as appropriate, in describing how the initial data were collected.

10 See *Introduction to Social Research* (Punch, 1988), pp. 94–104.

11 A general set of steps for doing this is shown in *Introduction to Social Research* (Punch, 1988), pp. 95–6.

12 See *Introduction to Social Research* (Punch, 1988), pp. 174–91.

13 As Punch (1994: 84) points out, much qualitative field research is dependent on one person's perception of the situation at a given point in time. That perception is shaped by personality and by the nature of the interaction with the researched. This makes the researcher his or her own 'research instrument'.

14 See *Introduction to Social Research* (Punch, 1988), pp. 104, 192.

15 Bell (1993: 58–9) has a useful checklist for negotiating access, which points to some of the common ethical issues in social research. This is a subject of increasing importance in the social research methods literature, a selection of which is indicated and overviewed in *Introduction to Social Research* (Punch, 1988: 281–2).

16 See *Introduction to Social Research* (Punch, 1988), pp. 111–37, 198–238.

6

Writing the Proposal

CONTENTS

6.1 INTRODUCTION

What should the research proposal as a finished product look like? What content should it include? What structure and sections might it have? This chapter deals first with these questions, bringing together what has been said in previous chapters, especially Chapter 5. It then comments on qualitative proposals.

In the literature, there are numerous descriptions of proposals, with suggestions and recommendations for proposal sections and headings. Sometimes these are written for social science research in general – examples are Madsen (1983), Behling (1984), Mauch and Birch (1989) and Peters (1997). Sometimes they are written for specific areas – examples here are Tornquist (1993) and Brink and Wood (1994) for nursing research, Borg and Gall (1989) and Krathwohl (1998) for educational research, Coley and Scheinberg (1990) for research in human services and the helping professions, Gitlin and Lyons (1996) for health research and human service professionals, Parsigian (1996) for media projects, and Hamper and Baugh (1996) for business research.

In addition, there is literature on 'grantsmanship' (research proposals for grant applications – see, for example, Lauffer, 1983, 1984; Gilpatrick, 1989), and literature on proposal preparation and development from within particular research approaches. Thus Marshall and Rossman (1989) and Maxwell (1996) write on proposals for qualitative research, while Locke et al. (1993) write mainly about proposals for quantitative research.

By contrast, the description of the research proposal given in this chapter aims to be general enough to suit different social science areas, and to cover quantitative, qualitative and mixed-method approaches to research. As noted earlier, it is written primarily with the dissertation student in mind, but I believe it has application also to the non-university context.

Before the proposal's sections and structure are discussed, it is worth noting again four points from previous chapters:

(a) Keep the framework of three overarching questions discussed in Chapter 3 in mind, since this will be what most of your readers are expecting your proposal to deal with. These are:

- What is this research trying to find out, what questions is it trying to answer?
- How will the proposed research answer these questions?
- Why is this research worth doing?

(b) Review again the five issues raised in Chapter 4. As noted there, they are not necessarily all applicable in any one project, but they are useful things to think about in planning the research and preparing the proposal. They are:

- the perspective behind the research;
- the role of theory;
- pre-structured vs unfolding research;
- the relevant literature;
- whether the study is to be quantitative, qualitative, or both.

When they do apply, how they are dealt with in the proposal is a matter of judgement for the writer – for example, whether, as points, they need a separate section, or are interwoven throughout other sections.

(c) Quoting Maxwell, remember that the form and structure of the proposal are tied to its purpose – '... to explain and justify your proposed study to an audience of nonexperts on your topic' (Maxwell, 1996: 100–1).

(d) The proposal itself needs to be presented as an argument. Seeing it as an argument means showing its line of reasoning, its internal consistency and the interrelatedness of its different parts. It means making sure that the different parts fit together, and showing how the research will be a piece of disciplined inquiry. As an argument, the proposal should show the logic behind the proposed study, rather than simply describing the study. In so doing, it should answer the question of why this approach, method and design have been chosen for this study.[1]

6.2   PROPOSAL HEADINGS[2]

In the interests of making the proposal clear and easy for the reader to follow, it will need an organizing framework, or structure. This section gives a suggested set of headings for writing and presenting the research proposal, shown in Box 6.1.

A problem in suggesting a general set of headings for proposals is the variation in headings, format and length of required documents across different areas of university research. There appear to be two extremes in university practice. Some universities (and some degrees) have institution-wide requirements, where the proposal covers the same headings in all disciplines. Other universities (and degrees) have department or area-specific requirements and headings.

Institution-wide formats are usually, and necessarily, more general. For example, they often use the broad heading 'aims' (or 'objectives'), rather than the more specific 'research questions' focus emphasized here. Again, the broad heading 'research plan' might be used, rather than the more specific term 'research methods'. Where these broader terms apply, the headings shown here in Box 6.1 can easily be clustered accordingly.

The focus in this book on empirical research in social science means that a common set of proposal headings should be broadly useful across areas. At the same time, there needs to be room for variability in proposal format, to reflect the variability in research approaches, while accommodating the general expectations a reader will have when reading the proposal. These headings address those expectations, but it follows that they are not necessarily the only sections or headings, nor is their suggested order the only one that could be used. Therefore, this description

BOX 6.1 *Checklist of headings for research proposals*

i.	Title and title page
ii.	Abstract
iii.	Introduction – Area and topic
	– Background and context
	– Statement of purpose (or aims)
iv.	Research questions – General
	– Specific
v.	Conceptual framework, theory, hypotheses (if appropriate)
vi.	The literature
vii.	Methods – Design – strategy and framework
	– Sample
	– Data collection – instruments and procedures
	– Data analysis
viii.	Significance
ix.	Limitations and delimitations (if appropriate)
x.	Consent, access and participants' protection
xi.	References
xii.	Appendices

is not meant to be prescriptive, and the researcher should feel at liberty to vary this material as appropriate. But that should be done against the background of readers' expectations (see Chapter 2), and any guidelines from the relevant department and/or university. Even if these particular headings are not used, the content they point to should be contained in the proposal, in some clear, easy-to-follow format.[3]

Some of these sections apply to both quantitative and qualitative research, whereas some are more directly applicable to one approach than the other. The writer's judgement is needed to decide which sections are appropriate, in which order, and which might be omitted or combined. But, as with the issues discussed in Chapter 4, the full list is useful to think about in proposal preparation, and is also useful for developing full versions of the proposal – where shorter versions are required, a good strategy is to prepare the full version, then summarize it. Also, the full version of the proposal, outlined here, will be useful when it comes to writing the dissertation itself.

It is easier in many respects to suggest proposal guidelines for a quantitative study, since there is greater variety in qualitative studies, and many qualitative studies will be unfolding rather than pre-structured. An unfolding study cannot be as specific in the proposal about its research questions, nor about details of the design. When this is the case, the point needs to be made in the proposal. Unfolding qualitative proposals are discussed again in Section 6.3.

Some proposals require the definition of terms. This occurs when terms are used which may not be understood by people outside the field of study, or when specialized technical terms are used, or when there is a need to define one or more terms clearly so that misunderstanding does not occur (Creswell, 1994: 106). Quantitative research in particular has a clear tradition of defining its variables, first conceptually and then operationally. Whether or not a separate section is required for any definition of terms is a matter of judgement – it can often easily be incorporated into other sections. But the conceptual and operational definition of variables in quantitative research is often best done in a separate section, perhaps under methods.

In what follows, I make some comments about abstracts and introductions. In the other main sections (research questions, conceptual framework, literature, methods), I bring together the points made in earlier chapters.

Abstract and title

An abstract is a brief summary, whether of a proposal or a finished study. It is *not* the introduction to a proposal or study, but rather a summary of it. It functions like the executive summary in the business context, giving readers a brief overview of all essential elements of the proposal.

Abstracts play an important role in the research literature, and they are required in proposals (usually), dissertations and in research articles in most refereed journals. Abstract writing is the skill of saying as much as possible in as few words as possible. For a proposal, the abstract needs to deal with two main issues – what the study is about and aims to achieve (usually stated in terms of its research questions), and how it intends to do that.[4] The abstract should give an overview not just of the study itself, but also of the argument behind the study.

For most of us, abstract writing is a skill which needs to be developed, since we typically use many superfluous words when we speak and write. Together with the title, the abstract is written last, since it is difficult to summarize what has not yet been written.

Examples of abstracts of proposals are difficult to find, since they are not collected and published. On the other hand, examples of abstracts of completed studies can be found in several places – completed dissertations, at the start of articles in many top class research journals, and in compilations of research such as Dissertation Abstracts International, and the various collections of abstracts in different social science areas.

Titles also have importance in the research literature indexing process. Therefore a title should not just be an afterthought, nor should it use words or phrases which obscure rather than reveal meaning. Extending the point about abstract writing, the title should convey as much information as possible in as few words as possible.

Introduction – area and topic, background and context and statement of purpose (or aims)

There are many ways a topic can be introduced, and all topics have a background and a context. These should be noted in the introduction, which sets the stage for the research. A strong introduction is important to a convincing proposal. It is the lead-in, to help the reader follow the logic of the proposal. Its purpose is not to review the literature, but rather to show generally how the proposed study fits into what is already known, and to locate it in relation to present knowledge and practice. Creswell (1994: 41) suggests four key components for introductions: (a) establishing the problem leading to the study, (b) casting the problem within the larger scholarly literature, (c) discussing deficiencies in the literature about the problem, and (d) targeting an audience and noting the significance of this problem for the audience.

In addition, I think the introduction should also contain a clear identification of the research area and topic, and a general statement of the purpose of the research.[5] These can lead later into general and specific research questions. Particular features of the proposed study, and important aspects of its context, can also be identified here, as appropriate – for example, if personal knowledge or experience form an important part of the context, or if preliminary or pilot studies have been done, or if the study will involve secondary analysis of existing data (Maxwell, 1996).

Especially for qualitative proposals, two other points might apply here. One is the first general issue raised in Chapter 4 – is there a particular perspective behind this research? This can be noted here, to inform the reader early in the proposal. The other is the third issue raised in Chapter 4 – where on the structure continuum is the proposed study? This strongly influences later sections of the proposal. If a pre-structured qualitative study is planned, the proposal can proceed along similar lines to the quantitative proposal. If an unfolding study is planned, where focus and structure will develop as the study proceeds, this point should be made clearly, again to inform the reader. In the former case, there will be general and specific research questions. In the latter case, there will be more general orienting research questions.

The introduction should be strong and engaging. Various logical structures are possible, but a progression from more general to more specific issues, culminating in stating the topic and research questions for this study, often works well. Whatever structure you choose, make sure your introduction actually does introduce your topic, and sets the stage for what follows. In my experience, it is a mistake for the introduction to go on too long, especially about the background to the research, and it is a good idea to get to the point of your research, stated as purpose in the introduction and leading on to research questions, as soon as is possible.

An excellent illustration of an introduction, with edited comments, is given by Creswell (1994: 45–8). Four others, also edited, are given in Locke et al. (1993: 185–296), and others in Gilpatrick (1989: 57–60).

Research questions – general and specific

The nature and central role of research questions were discussed in Chapter 3. In the proposal outline suggested here, they can follow from the statement of purpose given in the introduction. If your research questions fit into the general-to-specific framework described in Chapter 3, presenting them in the proposal in this section should be a quite straightforward matter. Remembering the empirical criterion for research questions in Chapter 3 (Section 3.6), it should be clear what data are required to answer each specific research question.

The point about this section is to tell the reader what questions the research is trying to answer, or what questions will initiate the inquiry in an unfolding study. This section is often what proposal readers turn to and concentrate on first, in order to get as clear a picture as possible of the purpose of the research. This reinforces the comments in Chapter 3 about the central role of research questions. It also implies that an emerging-unfolding type of study needs to indicate here what general questions will initiate the research, and how they might be refocused and refined as the study progresses.

Conceptual framework, theory and hypotheses (if appropriate)

There is wide variation in the applicability of this section, given the range of studies possible across the quantitative and qualitative approaches. If a conceptual framework is involved, it is a matter of judgement whether it goes here, or in the methods section later in the proposal. Theory and hypotheses are included if appropriate, as explained in Chapter 3. If theory is involved, it may be included in the literature review section, rather than here.

Thus, as noted in Chapter 4:

- if your study has a pre-determined conceptual framework, the proposal should show it; this can often be done effectively using a diagram;
- if this conceptual framework is seen as only an initial version or approximation, for modification as the study progresses, this should be noted when the framework is presented;
- if you have an unfolding study, where a conceptual framework will be developed during the research, this too should be noted and explained;
- the role of theory in the proposed study should be made clear. In particular, is it theory verification or theory generation? If a theory verification study is proposed, hypotheses, and the theory behind them should be shown.

The literature

The proposal needs to identify the body of literature which is relevant to the research, to indicate the relationship of the proposed study to the relevant literature, and to indicate how the literature will be dealt with in the proposed study. The following three possibilities were noted in Chapter 4.

- The literature is reviewed comprehensively in advance of the study, and that review is included as part of the proposal, or is attached.
- The literature will be reviewed comprehensively ahead of the empirical stage of the research, but that review will not be done until the proposal is approved. In this case, the nature and scope of the literature to be reviewed should be indicated.
- The literature will deliberately not be reviewed prior to the empirical work, but will be integrated into the research during the study, as in a grounded theory study. In this case too, the nature and scope of the literature should be indicated.

For some qualitative proposals, the literature may be used in sharpening the focus of the study, and to give structure to its questions and design.

If so, this should be indicated, along with how it is to be done. In all cases, the researcher needs to identify the relevant literature, and to connect the proposed study to the literature. In general, I agree with the advice of Locke et al. (1993) and Maxwell (1996) that the function of the literature *in the proposal* is to locate the present study, and to explain and justify the directions it proposes to take.

Methods

DESIGN – STRATEGY AND FRAMEWORK   At this point, the overall approach to be taken in the research – quantitative, qualitative, or both – becomes decisive. While this might well have been indicated earlier in the proposal, it is nonetheless useful to make it clear here (again, if necessary). Whichever approach applies, the proposal should identify the basic strategy behind the research. Thus:

- If the study is quantitative, what strategy is proposed?
- If qualitative, what strategy is proposed?
- If there is a combination of quantitative and qualitative approaches, what is the proposed mixture of strategies?

A clear statement of the strategy helps to orient the reader, and leads naturally to a description of the design.

The design connects the research questions to the data, and can now detail the implementation of the strategy. For example, if an experiment is planned, this section gives details of the proposed experimental design. If a case study is planned, this section gives details of the case study design – for example, single or multiple, cross sectional or longitudinal.

For conventional quantitative designs, the conceptual framework may be shown here, instead of earlier. In qualitative studies, the location of the study along the structure continuum is particularly important for its design. Qualitative strategies such as case studies, ethnography and grounded theory may overlap, or elements of these may be used separately or together. This means it will be difficult to neatly compartmentalize such a study. That is not a problem, but it should be made clear that the proposed study uses elements of different strategies. Qualitative studies vary greatly on the issue of pre-developed conceptual frameworks, and the position of the study on this matter should be indicated. A fully or partly pre-developed framework should be shown. Where one will be developed, it needs to be indicated how that will be done. This will interact with data collection and analysis, and may be better dealt with there.

Sample

Chapter 5 stressed the need to think about sampling in the study as part of the planning process for the research, to select among sampling possibilities in line with the logic of the study, and to indicate the sampling plan in the proposal. The rationale behind the sampling plan needs to fit in with the logic of the study, and to be briefly described. Whatever the approach, the basic idea in this section is to indicate who or what will be studied, and why.

If the study is quantitative, the proposal should indicate:

- the sampling strategy, especially whether it is purposive, representative or both, and what claims will be made for the generalizability of findings;
- how big the sample will be, and why;
- how it will be selected.

If the study is qualitative, the proposal should similarly indicate:

- the sampling strategy, including what intention (if any) there is for the generalizability of findings;
- the extent of the proposed sample;
- how sample units will be chosen.

If a case study is involved, the basis of case selection should be made clear, as should the basis of within-case sampling. If sampling of documentary or other qualitative material is proposed, its basis needs to be shown.

DATA COLLECTION   As indicated in Chapter 5, the two matters here are the instruments (if any) which will be used for data collection, and the procedures for administering the instruments or, more generally, for collecting the data.

(a) Instruments for quantitative data collection:

- If the decision is to use already-existing data collection instruments, a brief description of their history, use in research and their basic psychometric characteristics (especially reliability and validity information, if available) should be included.
- If the decision is to construct an instrument(s) specifically for this study, an outline of the steps involved in doing that should be given, showing what pre-testing is involved.

(b) Instruments for qualitative data collection:

- A general plan for any qualitative fieldwork should be shown; if the researcher is the 'instrument' for data collection, the proposal should indicate this.
- If interviews are involved what type of interviews, and especially, what degree of structure and standardization is proposed? If standardized interview schedules are to be used, how will they be developed and pre-tested?

- If qualitative questionnaires are proposed, what degree of structure and standardization is involved? How would they be developed and (if appropriate) pre-tested?
- Similar considerations apply for observational data – what degree of structure and standardization is proposed, and how would proposed schedules be developed and pre-tested?
- If documents are to be used, which ones and why? Are there sampling or access considerations?
- If diaries, journals, critical incident reports, or other qualitative materials are involved, how would the collection of these, including any sampling aspects, be organized?

(c) Procedures – for both quantitative and qualitative approaches, the proposal needs to indicate:

- how the data will be collected;
- how the proposed procedures are arranged to maximize the quality of the data.

Issues of access and ethics may be dealt with here, if they apply especially to data collection procedures, or in the section on consent, access and participants' protection, if they apply more generally.

DATA ANALYSIS   The objective in this section is to indicate how the data will be analysed. Quantitative proposals should indicate the statistical procedures proposed. Similarly, the qualitative proposal needs to show how its data will be analysed, and how the proposed analysis fits with the other components of the study. If applicable, both types of proposal should indicate what computer use is planned in the analysis of the data. As noted in Chapter 5, this is an area where you may well need the help of an expert.

Significance

Here, the proposal should indicate the significance of the proposed study. Synonyms for 'significance' here might be justification, importance, or contribution of the study. They all address the third general question of Chapter 3: why is this study worth doing? While the particular topic and its context will determine a study's significance, there are three general areas for the significance and contribution of a study: to knowledge in the area, to policy considerations and to practitioners (Marshall and Rossman, 1989). The first of these, contribution to knowledge, is closely tied to the literature in the area, and is often interpreted as theoretical contribution. If the study has the clear objective of theory generation or verification, indicating this contribution is straightforward.

Limitations and delimitations (if appropriate)

'Limitations' refer to limiting conditions or 'restrictive weaknesses' (Locke et al., 1993: 18) which are unavoidably present in the study's design. Any study has limitations, and they should be noted in the proposal, which should argue nonetheless for the importance of this work. 'Delimitations' means defining the limits, or drawing the boundaries around a study, and showing clearly what is and is not included. This is sometimes useful in avoiding misunderstanding by the reader.

Consent, access and participants' protection

All social research involves consent, access and associated ethical issues, since it is based on data from people and about people. Section 5.3.4, on data collection procedures, shows a range of different ethical issues which might arise in research. Some ethical issues are present in almost all projects (for example, anonymity and confidentiality of data, the use of results), while others are much more project-specific (for example, intervention and advocacy). The researcher needs to anticipate the particular ethical issues involved in the proposed project, and to indicate in the proposal how they will be dealt with.

References

This is a list of the references cited in the proposal.

Appendices

These may include any of the following: a timetable for the research, a budget for the research, letters of introduction or permission, consent forms, measuring instruments, questionnaires, interview guides, observation schedules, and examples of pilot study or other relevant work already completed (Maxwell, 1996).

6.3 QUALITATIVE PROPOSALS

Qualitative studies vary greatly, and in many, the design and procedures will evolve. As noted earlier, this obviously means that the proposal writer cannot specify exactly what will be done, in contrast to many quantitative proposals. When this is the case, the proposal can explain the flexibility the study requires, and show how decisions will be made as the study unfolds. Together with this, as much detail as possible should be provided. Review committees have to judge both the quality, feasibility and viability of the proposed project, and the ability of the researcher to carry it out. The proposal itself, through its organization, coherence and integration, attention to detail and conceptual clarity can inspire confidence in the researcher's ability to execute the research.

On the one hand then, for some types of qualitative research especially, we do not want to constrain too much the structure of the proposal, and we need to preserve flexibility. On the other hand, as pointed out in Section 4.3, this does not mean that 'anything goes'. Eisner (1991: 241–2) writes as follows, about qualitative research in education:

> Qualitative research proposals should have a full description of the topic to be investigated, a presentation and analysis of the research relevant to that topic, and a discussion of the issues within the topic or the shortfalls within the research literature that make the researcher's topic a significant one. They should describe the kinds of information that are able to be secured and the variety of methods or techniques that will be employed to secure such information. The proposals should identify the kinds of theoretical or explanatory resources that might be used in interpreting what has been described, and describe the kind of places, people, and materials that are likely to be addressed.
>
> The function of proposals is not to provide a watertight blueprint or formula the researcher is to follow, but to develop a cogent case that makes it plain to a knowledgeable reader that the writer has the necessary background to do the study and has thought clearly about the resources that are likely to be used in doing the study, and that the topic, problem, or issue being addressed is educationally significant.

This elaborates Eisner's earlier comments (see Section 4.3) that 'evidence matters' and 'planning is necessary'. I want now to extend these points, focusing both on proposals for qualitative research in general, and in particular on those with unfolding rather than pre-structured elements. This sort of proposal is probably the most difficult to write, but the following points can guide the writing. They fit in with the headings shown in Box 6.1, though some modifications are required.

First, there should still be an identification of the research area and topic, and an introduction to those which places them in context and describes any necessary aspects of the background to the study. Second, there still needs to be an identification of the relevant literature, a connection of the proposed study to that literature, and an indication of how the research itself will deal with the literature. Third, there needs to be an assessment of the proposed study's significance and contribution, including its contribution in relation to the literature.

Fourth, when it comes to research questions, it is likely that only general guiding and starting research questions will be identified in such a proposal, supported by statements as to why this is appropriate and as to how more-specific questions to direct the investigation will be identified as the research proceeds. As a matter of proposal presentation strategy, it is a good idea to indicate possible (or likely) research questions as the study unfolds, while pointing out that they are first approximations, to be revised and changed as the study proceeds. It is usually not difficult to make an intelligent first approximation to the sorts of research questions that might arise, through anticipating, and trying to imagine or simulate the research situation. For some research also, some small-scale empirical exploration (or pilot study) may be possible in developing the proposal. Where possible, this is very helpful in keeping things grounded.

Fifth, when it comes to design and methods, there should be clear statements in the proposal about the general research strategy envisaged, about the sorts of empirical materials to be targeted (at least initially), and about the general plan for collecting and analysing them. As before, the description of methods should not stop at a general identification of the research strategy. The proposal needs also to indicate awareness of the procedural and methodological choices ahead of the researcher in implementing the general strategy, and the basis on which those choices will be made. This was the distinction made in Section 5.3.1 between general and procedural descriptions of methods. Terms describing qualitative research strategies such as the case study, or participant observation, or grounded theory, or an interview-based study, are necessary but generic descriptions, identifying an approach and a strategy in general terms. The execution of any of these in research involves numerous procedural and methodological choices. Thus the 'interview-based study', for example, involves choices about such matters as the selection of interview respondents, approaches to them, the establishment of trust and rapport, physical arrangements for the interview (time, place, etc.), recording procedures, the type of interview, the nature of the questions and the role (if any) of an interview schedule and pre-testing. The qualitative proposal does not need to be able to answer all such questions. Indeed, many of them may well be unanswerable, at proposal stage. But the proposal should indicate awareness of such upcoming methodological choices, and the basis on which they will be made.

Sixth, the other proposal headings listed (abstract and title, limitations and delimitations, consent, access and participants' protection, references and appendices) apply, as appropriate, as before.

Writing the proposal for a qualitative study can be more complicated, given the less pre-structured nature of most such research. The writer should indicate early in the document the unfolding nature of the proposed research and why such an approach is appropriate for this study on this topic in this context at this time. The need to preserve flexibility, the unfolding nature of the study, and the ways in which this research will follow a path of discovery can be strongly stated. Against that background, it is good advice to develop likely research questions and issues of design and methods as far as possible in the proposal, indicating what methodological choices will be involved and the basis on which they will be made.

NOTES

1 Maxwell (1996: 112–13) has an excellent example showing the structure of a dissertation proposal, as an argument with its own logic. Locke et al. (1993: 18) suggest three useful questions which address the logic of the proposed research, its topic and research question: what do we already know or do? (The purpose here, in one or two sentences, is to support the legitimacy and importance of the question.) How does this particular question relate to what we already know or do? (The purpose here is to explain and support the exact form of questions or hypotheses that serve as the focus for the study.) Why select this particular method of investigation? (The purpose here is to explain and support the selections made from among alternative methods of investigation.)

2 See *Introduction to Social Research* (Punch, 1988), pp. 268–79.

3 Other lists of possible proposal headings are shown in the literature noted in the introduction to this chapter, and other proposal outlines are described by Morse (1994) and by Kelly (1998).

4 For a finished report (or dissertation), the abstract would need to deal with three issues – these two, and a third which summarizes what was found.

5 Creswell (1994: 56–67) gives examples of purpose statements for five different types of studies – a phenomenological study, a case study, an ethnographic study, a grounded theory study and a quantitative survey.

Tactics

CONTENTS

7.1 INTRODUCTION

I believe there is no one way to develop a research proposal, and I have seen how much difference there is between the way different researchers proceed.[1] But I have also found that some strategies and tactics are consistently useful, especially for student researchers coming to proposal development for the first time. This chapter presents those. Before that, however, I restate what I see as five general tactical considerations, which I think should stay in the proposal writer's mind throughout the process of proposal development. They follow on from what has been said in previous chapters.

7.2 GENERAL TACTICAL ISSUES

(a) Keep an overall focus on the three general questions:

- *What* am I trying to find out?
- *How* am I going to do it?
- *Why* is this worth doing?

(b) Put the 'what' question before the 'how' question. As far as possible, make research methods dependent on research questions, rather than questions dependent on methods. Remember that how you ask questions has implications for the methods to use in finding answers to them.

(c) Realize that you will almost certainly have to re-visit both questions (the 'what' and the 'how' questions) several times before you get the proposal right. The process is an iterative one, whether the proposal is quantitative, qualitative, or mixed-method. Whereas the research proposal, as a product, is expected to be neat, tidy, well-structured and interconnected, showing clarity and internal consistency, the process, by contrast, is usually messy, iterative, stop-start, and often punctuated with tensions, hesitations and contradictions. The same is true of much of research itself.[2]

(d) The importance of feedback: throughout the process of putting your proposal together, you will need reactions and feedback from various quarters – friends, fellow students, and especially supervisors. Make it easy for them to give you feedback which helps. Two ways you can do that are to provide them with draft documents which are easily understood, and to raise directly with them (preferably attached to your drafts) questions and matters on which you would like their reaction.

(e) Modularizing: student researchers are often daunted by the task of producing a finished research proposal. It can seem formidable. But, like other formidable tasks, it loses much of its sting when broken down into smaller, specific, component tasks. To do that requires an outline, and Chapter 6 suggests sections for that outline. Once the outline is in place, even if provisionally, you can begin assembling and categorizing your notes into these sections and organizing these into points to be made. From this basis, the writing itself can begin. Modularizing the work this way is one of the great benefits of having a structured outline, with sections (or modules). That outline itself may well be developed iteratively.

Against the background of these general considerations, I now have some specific tactical suggestions to add to those discussed in Section 3.7.

7.3 DEPARTMENTAL (OR UNIVERSITY) GUIDELINES

No matter how obvious it seems, an important tactical issue right at the start of proposal development is to find out what departmental and/or university guidelines, regulations and policies apply, both to the proposal and to the final dissertation. Locke et al. (1993: 5–6) note that there will usually be three main sources of regulation: 'Normally, the planning and execution of student research are circumscribed by existing departmental policy on format for the final report, university regulations concerning thesis and dissertation reports, and informal standards exercised by individual advisors or study committees'.

They point out also that there is wide variation in specificity between departments and universities. Some regulations are very explicit ('the proposal may not exceed 25 typewritten pages', or 'the proposal will conform to the style established in the Publication Manual of the American Psychological Association'), whereas others are very general ('the research topic must be of suitable proportions', or 'the proposal must reflect a thorough knowledge of the problem area').

As well as checking on departmental and/or university and/or dissertation committee regulations and guidelines regarding the proposal, it is useful also to find out about the process of proposal evaluation and approval in your department, and, if possible, to consult previous successful proposals. You can learn a lot from reading these, and it also usually makes your task seem less formidable.[3]

Time and length guidelines might be laid down, and increasingly, universities are placing size limits on proposals and dissertations. Two main reasons for this are that the sheer volume of research going on today demands some limit on the size of proposals (and reports), and that a strong argument can be made that it is good discipline to be able to describe the proposed research (or completed project) in a certain limited number of words (or pages). According to this argument, it is important to develop the skill to say what you need to say about your research within these limits of time and length.

On the other hand, to give a full treatment of all the issues raised in this book (including, as appropriate, those in Chapter 4) may well require a proposal document which might exceed these limits. What to do in these cases? A good way to handle this situation is to prepare a full version, along the lines described here, and then to summarize it down to the required length. This shows the review committee that you have done a thorough job in proposal preparation (you can indicate in your shortened version that a full version is available, and perhaps also include parts of it as an appendix). But also, the full version of the proposal will be an important contribution to the final dissertation itself. After the proposal is approved and the research is executed, you will have to report it in a dissertation. That dissertation is expected to be a full and detailed report of the research, though again, it will be expected to conform to size limits. Much of what is written in the full version of the proposal can be imported directly into the final dissertation.

7.4 GETTING STARTED

Getting started in developing a proposal means either being able to identify a research area and topic, and moving towards general and specific questions within that topic, or knowing the specific research question(s) of interest, and being able to locate those within more general questions, a topic and area.

Many writers have discussed ways of getting started in research, and the sources and types of research areas and topics. Examples are the writings of Marshall and Rossman (1989), Campbell et al. (1982) and Zuckerman (1978). Neuman (1994: 110) suggests seven ways of selecting topics[4] and Gitlin and Lyons (1996: 36) discuss seven different sources of ideas for funding.[5] Locke et al. (1993: 48) suggest that research questions emerge from three broad sources: logic, practicality and accident. As good practical advice for beginning research students, they also recommend the benefits of conversing with peers, listening to professorial discussions, assisting in research projects, attending lectures and conferences, exchanging papers and corresponding with faculty and students at other institutions.

Other writers suggest other 'getting started' ideas. Thus, Mauch and Birch (1989: 43–55) discuss choosing topics, and assessing the feasibility and appropriateness of topics. Peters (1997: 179–90) writes on 'finding your thesis topic', and Madsen (1983: 20–34) writes on 'selecting and shaping your research topic'. Maxwell (1996: 24) has a writing exercise on 'reflecting on your purposes' and a little later (1996: 47–8) an exercise for creating a concept map. Calnan (1984: 19–21) has five preliminary tests for research ideas: the writing test, the credibility test, the friendly colleague test, the freshness test and the possibility test.

Thus there is no shortage of literature on sources for research ideas, and I do not want to add to that. But I do want to stress here that the identification of a research area and topic is not a trivial decision, for two reasons. One is that much has been accomplished when an area and topic have been selected. That selection gives a clear focus to subsequent work, and enables you to connect your project to the literature. Of course, identifying the area and topic are only the first steps, and you need to go further, by developing both general and specific research questions. But a big step forward has been taken when this has been done.

The other reason is that you will be working on your research topic for a sustained period, investing in it a substantial amount of your time and other resources (both intellectual and emotional!). Therefore it is good that your motivation and interest be high for the topic and questions you are considering. 'Inadequately motivated research tends not to be completed or, worse, is finished in a pedestrian fashion far below the student's real capacity' (Locke et al., 1993: 44). This suggests another important criterion in selecting your research area and topic – make sure you have a genuine and sustainable interest in it.

7.4.1 The 'two pager'

Often a good way to formalize getting started, after some period of work, is to write *no more than two pages*, describing, as clearly and directly as possible, what the proposed research is trying to find out, and how it will do it. Students usually have some difficulty doing this. I find that common faults are for the one or two pages to expand to five, six, or ten, and for the focus to be on the context, background and literature somehow relevant to the issue, rather than the issue itself – the 'what' and the 'how' of the proposed research. These things – the context, background and literature – of course have their place. But the value of this exercise, at this point, is in forcing a confrontation with the central questions of 'what am I trying to find out?' and 'how am I going to do it?' and in that order. Limiting this document to two pages is a deliberate strategy to get past the context and background.

Like other stages in proposal development, getting satisfactory and stable answers to these questions is inevitably an iterative process. It takes several tries, and almost nobody gets it right the first time. In any case, the two-pager is a work-in-progress document. Its function is to see where your thinking is up to, so you can take it to the next stage. Its benefit is to get systematic thinking started, and to ensure an early focus on writing, with these central questions in mind.

As a supervisor, I most often find that discussing a first attempt at this two-pager with the student leads naturally to a second (and sometimes third and fourth) attempt, and that these attempts progressively produce a clearer initial statement. Once that is in place, even if tentatively, it provides the springboard for the next stage of thinking, reading and discussing. You can see what you need to do next.

7.4.2 The ideas paper

Another useful strategy, sometimes instead of the two-pager, sometimes alongside it, is to write an ideas paper, which sets out to sketch the context and background to the proposed topic, and which probably deals also with some of the main themes in the literature. A primary purpose here is to identify main issues, points or themes, with a view to proceeding more or less deductively from these to research questions. When progress is not deductive, but more interactive, moving backwards and forwards between general and specific issues, the ideas paper can have value in stimulating this. The trick is not to let it become the main focus of this stage of work, but to use it to lead into the central 'what' and 'how' questions.

What I call here an 'ideas paper' is sometimes called a 'preliminary discussion paper' or a 'discussion and concept paper' (Gilpatrick, 1989: 45, 101). These labels and interpretations are often valuable for the researcher who focuses on the problem rather than the question (see Section 2.6). Whatever they might be called, such papers will normally bring the benefits of helping you to sort out your ideas on a topic, indicating and perhaps starting to draw on relevant literature (what do others know or say about this topic?), and bringing into focus what you already know about the topic, perhaps from an experiential base.

7.4.3 Working deductively

If you are stuck, or are having trouble organizing your ideas and making them systematic, referring again to the hierarchy of concepts in Chapter 3 can help. From the most general to the most specific, that hierarchy is: research area, research topic, general research questions, specific research questions, data collection questions. We can develop from that hierarchy a simple set of deductive steps for developing a research proposal. Thus, for example, a six-step model is to:

- select a research area;
- develop one or more topics within that area;
- select one from among these topics to keep your project manageable;
- develop research questions, general and specific, for this topic;
- determine what data would be required to answer each specific research question;
- select research design, data collection and data analysis procedures in order to do this.

The value of this sort of thinking is not as a lock-step, formula-like approach to research planning. Rather, it is a useful 'fall-back' frame of reference for an overloaded or confused research planner. And you do not have to start this process from the top and work down. You can start from the middle – for example, with a particular specific research question of interest – and then move up and down the set of steps, up and down the hierarchy of concepts as appropriate.

7.5 THE VALUE OF DISCUSSION

Ultimately, in its written form, the proposal goes to some wider audience. At that stage, as noted earlier, the ideal completed proposal is a stand-alone document, able to be read and understood (and, in due course, approved) by a mixture of expert and non-expert readers. A valuable step, on the way to that, is discussing your developing ideas. Discussing is itself a process, in miniature, of taking your work to a wider audience.

Discussion with whom? In my opinion, with anybody at all that you find helpful – but especially with your supervisor(s), with other research students and/or colleagues and/or others working in similar areas, and with non-expert friends, acquaintances and so on. This last type of discussant, being non-expert, might play the very valuable role of the 'naïve inquirer'.

Discussing your developing proposal has several benefits for your work:

- It is a step towards writing things down; both discussing your ideas with others and writing them down force you to think about stucturing and representing your ideas so that they can be understood by others.
- It is a part of the clarification/communication process – you have both to plan and design a piece of research, and communicate that plan to others.
- It brings feedback from others, which is often important in clarification.
- It may suggest aspects of, or perspectives on, your topic that have so far escaped you.
- Discussion with experts may suggest literature you need to consult; discussion with non-experts may suggest aspects of the context or situation you need to take into account.

7.6 THE VALUE OF WRITING IT DOWN

'Like the turtle, we progress only with our necks stuck out.' This is often good advice on proposal development. Translated, it means: have a go at writing your ideas down, especially if you are stuck, or if you are at a point where you have done quite a lot of reading and thinking and it is time to try to capture, consolidate and order your ideas. You do this sort of writing 'as best as you can see things at the moment', knowing that this is a draft, a step on the way to a finished product. This exercise will throw up points and issues that need more thought, discussion, or reading. As before, the structuring and representation of ideas are involved here, as is the relationship between thinking and writing. Thus the main value of the concrete activity of writing it down, for someone else to read, is in clarification. This is an example of 'writing to learn' as discussed in *Introduction to Social Research* (Punch, 1998: Ch. 12). More specifically, it is an example of writing in order to sort things out.

7.7 THREE COMMON DILEMMAS

This section deals with three dilemmas which often occur as students develop proposals. The first is the problem of several topics at once, the second is getting to closure versus getting to closure too quickly, the third is focusing on the context, background and literature versus focusing on the research questions. I think of these as tensions in the research planning process, which are almost inevitable as work on the proposal progresses.

7.7.1 Several topics at once

I have already noted that one common problem students experience is selecting a research area and topic, and getting the development of the proposal started. But another common problem is finding that there is more than one topic (or proposal, or project) emerging, as the student continues to work. There are two main versions of this problem. One is deciding among possible research areas and topics. The other is deciding among possible research questions, after the area and topic have been selected.

A situation frequently encountered is where the student can see more than one, and perhaps several, attractive research areas and questions. These may be related to each other, or they may be rather unconnected and discrete. This situation is most common early in the process of developing the proposal. As Brink and Wood (1993: xii) say: 'Perhaps the hardest task of all is deciding on one well-defined topic. There is so much to do that it is hard not to want to do it all at once'.

Faced with this problem, one strategy to consider is to develop more than one idea, as a possible proposal, up to a certain point. Most of the time, none of us can see clearly, up-front and in advance of a certain amount of work, where any one topic or set of questions might lead. Therefore, instead of trying to make judgements too early, it is better to push ahead with more than one topic for a period of time, in order to see where each leads – what type of study each leads to, how feasible and 'do-able' each is, how each fits with the interests, preferences and situation of the student, and so on. The two-pager is helpful here. Of course there comes a time when judgements are needed as to future directions, and decisions have to be made. The point here is that keeping the options open for a time, while more than one area is explored, is often good policy.

The second aspect of this problem is when we discover, through the question development stage, that an initial apparently quite straightforward topic has much more in it than first meets the eye. This is by no means uncommon, and we usually only get to see this by developing the topic and its questions to a reasonable extent.

What generally happens after a period of question development (see Section 3.7.1) is that the project has expanded, sometimes greatly. This can cause anxiety, but for most projects it should happen. In fact, if it doesn't, we should probably be concerned, since it may be a sign of insufficient question development work. Therefore, it is to be encouraged, within reason, as an important stage. Probing, exploring and seeing other possibilities with a topic can be valuable before reaching closure on the specific directions for a project.

When a small set of starting questions has multiplied into a larger set, disentangling and ordering are required. Disentangling is necessary because one question will often have other questions within it. Ordering involves categorizing, and the grouping of questions together. This will soon become hierarchical, and general and specific research questions begin to be distinguishable from each other.

The final stage then involves bringing the project down to size, since it has usually become too big. In fact, it probably suggests a research programme with several research projects by now. How is this trimming done? It involves deciding which questions are manageable within the practical constraints of this project, and which seem the most central and important. There are of course limits around any project – even if that project involves a grant and a team of researchers. The principle here is that it is better to do a smaller project thoroughly than a larger project superficially. Trimming a project down to size is a matter of judgement, and experience in research has a big role to play here. Once again, therefore, this stage is best done in collaboration with others. This stage is sometimes called delimiting the project. This means drawing the boundaries around it, and showing what is not in the project, as well as what is.

How many research questions should there be? There are practical limitations on any one project, and, as noted, it is better to have a small job done thoroughly than a large job done only superficially. More than about three or four general research questions, assuming that each is subdivided into specific questions, is testing the upper limit of what can be done in one study.

7.7.2 Getting to closure versus getting to closure too quickly

Many higher degree programmes have a mixture of course work and research dissertation. Completing the coursework is not normally the problem for most higher degree students. Completing the dissertation sometimes is.[6] The first major step in completing the dissertation is to complete the research proposal, and have it accepted.

For some students, the process of choosing a research area and topic, pondering its complexities, mastering its literature, and formulating questions and methods to guide the investigation, can take too long. Indeed, as with the dissertation itself, there is a time limit usually imposed on this stage of the work. This reflects the view noted earlier, that part of the task is to get the job (proposal or dissertation) done within a certain period of time, and to get the story told within a certain number of words.

This means that there is a point at which, after an appropriate period of time, consideration and work, it is necessary to make decisions and complete the proposal. It is necessary to 'get to closure'. It helps in doing this to remember:

- that there is no such thing as a perfect research proposal (or dissertation);
- that it is appropriate to be aware of, and to make the reader aware of, difficulties, problems and limitations, while not being overly defensive about the research;
- that not all of the issues which might arise in a piece of research have to be dealt with in the proposal; some might well be dealt with after acceptance of the proposal, in the execution stage of the research itself. In these cases, they should be noted in the proposal;
- that emergent and unfolding designs will naturally be less definitive at the proposal stage than those which take a highly pre-planned and pre-structured approach.[7]

However, while some students have trouble getting to closure, there is also the opposite problem of getting to closure too quickly. That is why the phrase 'after an appropriate period of time' was used above. During this planning stage, there is some benefit to hastening slowly. Since research questions do not usually come out right the first time, several iterations are often required, and we only reach a full answer to the question 'What are we trying to find out?' after careful thought. This question development stage needs time – time to see the possible questions buried in an area and to see related questions which follow from an analysis of particular questions. The theme in Section 3.7.1 was the importance of the pre-empirical, setting-up stage of the research – the decisions taken here will influence what is done in later stages. This does not mean that the decisions cannot be varied, as when iteration towards the final research questions goes on during the early empirical stages of the project. But varying them should not be done lightly if considerable effort has been invested in reaching them during the set-up stage.

7.7.3 Focus on context, background and literature versus focus on research questions

Clearly, both context, background and literature on the one hand, and research questions on the other, are necessary in the finished proposal (or dissertation). So it is not a question of one of these things or the other. The question here is about the focus on each, and especially about the timing of the focus on each, in developing the proposal.

On the one hand, focusing too much on the context, background and the literature too early in the process of research planning can result in lengthy essays on these topics, delaying (sometimes almost indefinitely) the proposal itself. It can also strongly affect the direction of the research, not always beneficially. On the other hand, focusing only on the research questions runs the risk of unnecessary, uninformed and inappropriate duplication of research, and/or of decontextualizing the research.

The solution, as usual, is a matter of judgement, in how the two things are balanced and integrated. Some of both is essential, and I do not believe a formula can be prescribed for general use. With some topics, approaches and students, it is appropriate to focus heavily on research questions and methods until major directions for the research have been set. With others, it is important to get the context, background and literature integrated into the thinking early.

At the same time, I often feel that the danger of a student being overwhelmed by, or at least strongly influenced by, the literature especially, and to a lesser extent being preoccupied with matters of context and background, can be worse than the danger of developing research questions in isolation from literature, context and background. I think this is especially true in applied social science areas, where the student often brings important knowledge[8] to the research. I do not believe that knowledge should be ignored.

That is why I usually recommend focusing, first, on the what and how of the research, and then fitting context, background and literature around that. But the process is, overall, interactive. And, for most proposals, the writer moves backwards and forwards between the context–background–literature and the research questions, as the proposal develops.

7.8 THE IMPORTANCE OF CLARITY

Finally, and as noted several times already, your proposal will be much more convincing if it is clear. The following two main ideas are involved in achieving this.

- Organizing for understanding: the proposal will be easier for readers to understand, especially in the stand-alone context described, if it is structured in a logical and coherent way. This means there should be clearly identified sections, which together cover the material expected, and which are suitably interconnected with each other. It also means that, as a writer, you are putting yourself in the position of the reader, and anticipating reader reactions;
- Writing for clarity: much has been written on this topic, and there are many strategies, tips, hints and lists of 'do's and 'don't's in the literature.[9] Writing for the academic research context (proposal or dissertation or, later on, journal articles) demands both acceptable scholarly

format and clarity. Both, and especially the latter, take time. Good writing, in this context, is invariably the result of drafting and redrafting, sharpening and shortening. I agree with the phrase used by Locke et al. (1993: 46) when they suggest the need for 'semantic and conceptual hygiene'. Your thinking in a research situation needs to be systematic, organized and disciplined. Your writing needs to reflect that. Semantic and conceptual hygiene should lead on to linguistic hygiene.

7.9 EXAMPLES OF PROPOSALS

I include here two examples of proposals, one quantitative and one qualitative. Both are from educational research, the field where I mostly work. But a caveat is now required. I have tried to write this as a general book for developing social science research proposals, without wishing to favour one style or type or approach over others. Since space reasons make it impossible to have proposals of all different types in this one book, any selection runs the risk of appearing to favour one sort of research over another, or of suggesting a 'template' for students to follow (Maxwell, 1996: 116). That is not intended. Rather, they are included as examples of best practice, and they are included here without comment. They illustrate many of the points made in earlier chapters.

These two proposals are presented in full. Coming after them, there is also a list of examples of other proposals in the literature. That list gives an idea of the range and diversity of proposals, with titles included where available to indicate the area and topic of the research.

Both full proposals are for the doctoral research at The University of Western Australia. As noted in Section 6.2, proposal requirements here are institution-wide, with the general heading of Proposed Study and Research Plan covering headings (iii) through to (vii) in Box 6.1. The University of Western Australia also asks candidates in their proposal to address the way in which the proposed research will meet the doctoral criterion of a 'substantial and original contribution to knowledge', and that section is included here. Other proposal headings less relevant to this book are omitted from the versions of the proposal shown here, as are details of references.[10]

[a] QUANTITATIVE PROPOSAL

Name of Candidate: Nola Purdie

Degree: Doctor of Philosophy, The University of Western Australia

A. Proposed Study

(i) Title

A cross-cultural investigation of the relationship between student conceptions of learning and their use of self-regulated learning strategies.

(ii) Aims

For a variety of reasons there is an increasing number of overseas students, particularly from south-east Asian countries, who are being educated in Australian schools. Differences in schooling and cultural traditions lead to different understandings of what learning actually is and to the strategies students use to regulate their own learning. Although it is not possible to speak with accuracy of an 'Asian' culture, it is, nevertheless, possible to identify several cultural characteristics that strongly influence understandings and practices related to education and learning that appear to be common across a number of Asian countries (Biggs, 1991; Garner, 1991; Hess & Azume, 1991; Thomas, 1990). In particular, concepts of filial piety and self-control, and an emphasis on rote memorization as a way of learning, contrast strongly with the qualities of independence of thought, verbal assertiveness, and learning through the development of meaning which are promoted as desirable behaviours in Australian students. If Australian teachers are to cater successfully for students from other cultures, it is important that we develop a better understanding of what these students actually think learning is and how they go about doing it.

This research, therefore, aims to determine if cultural differences in understandings about the nature of learning and the strategies used by students to perform a range of academic tasks do exist. Specifically, the research will compare the conceptions of learning and the use of self-regulated learning strategies of Australian secondary school students for whom English is a first language with those of students from two different south-east Asian countries (hereafter referred to collectively as Asian students). The research will test the hypothesis that what students understand by learning will, to a certain extent, determine their use of self-regulated learning strategies.

It is expected that the experience of schooling in Australia will cause changes in understandings about the nature of learning and the use of learning strategies. To investigate these changes, comparisons will be made between Asian students before they have been exposed to schooling in Australia and Asian students who have had several years of education in Australia and for whom English is a second language. The relationship between the level of English language proficiency of the Asian students and their use of self-regulated learning strategies will also be explored.

(iii) This study's substantial and original contribution to knowledge

The proposed research represents a substantial and original contribution to knowledge in that a cross-cultural perspective will be taken with respect to the investigation of students' conceptions of learning and their use of learning strategies. The research project will extend and integrate theory and findings from several areas of research relating to student learning. Self-regulated learning theory, developed through research from Western participants, will be applied to participants from two different south-east Asian countries. The motivational component of self-regulated learning will be explored with a view to expanding the already established output notion of what prompts students to engage in self-regulated learning to include an input component. Finally, theory that suggests that second language competence may be a factor in student use of self-regulated learning strategies will be tested.

(iv)   Theoretical framework

Introduction

The importance of self-regulation in learning has now been firmly established (Bandura, 1989; Zimmerman, 1990b). In contrast to investigations of student achievement that focus on student ability as the key factor in learning, self-regulation theory focuses attention on *why* and *how* students become initiators and controllers of their own learning. *How* students self-regulate has largely been explained by the degree to which a student is aware of and uses appropriately specific strategies to achieve their academic goals. The *why* of self-regulation has been explained in terms of motivational processes that are dependent on learning outcomes which have either tangible or intangible personal implications. 'Behaviorally oriented approaches focus on tangible outcomes such as material or social gains, whereas cognitively oriented approaches emphasize intangible outcomes such as self-actualization, self-efficacy, or reduced cognitive dissonance' (Zimmerman, 1990, p. 11).

The proposed research seeks to extend this view of motivational causation to include another component. In current theory, outcomes, both tangible and intangible, are considered to be the prime motivators of self-regulation in learning. A theory will be developed that posits inputs as an important, additional motivational factor. Specifically, input is that which students bring to academic tasks thereby prompting them to be proactive and systematic controllers of the learning process. In contrast to outcomes, where the focus is on a future-oriented actuality, inputs are derived from past experiences and are very much active in the present. Although there are bound to be several different sources of inputs, this research will focus on just one – student conceptions of learning. It will be argued, and subsequently tested, that what students understand by learning will, to a certain extent, determine their use of self-regulated learning strategies.

Self-regulated learning

Many studies have established the relationship between achievement, strategy use, and verbal self-efficacy in self-regulated learning (e.g. Bandura, 1982; Schunk, 1984; Zimmerman and Martinez-Pons, 1986, 1990) but this research has used Western participants for whom English is their first language. There are two potential problems with generalizing from these studies to second language users from a non-Western background. First, there may not be cross-cultural conceptual equivalence regarding the notion of self-regulated learning; and second, competence in the use of English may influence a student's ability to use self-regulated learning strategies, particularly those which are, in part, dependent on the four macro language skills of speaking, listening, reading and writing.

Self-regulation theory evolved out of an understanding of self-control as the product of socialization processes aimed at the development of moral standards of conduct (Bandura, 1977). Zimmerman (1990) noted Bandura's later extension of this theory to include a goal-related aspect. A person's goals and expectations are seen to provide the motivational stimulus to the self-control of behaviour which is directed at effecting changes in self or situation.

One current theory of self-regulated learning perceives students to be self-regulated learners to the extent that they are metacognitively, motivationally and behaviourally active participants in their own learning processes (Zimmerman, 1986). This theory proposes that self-regulated learning involves three key elements: use of self-regulated learning strategies, self-efficacy perceptions of performance skill, and commitment to academic goals (Zimmerman, 1990). Self-regulated learning strategies involve agency, purpose and instrumentality self-perceptions by a learner and are aimed at acquiring information and skill. Furthermore, this theory proposes triad reciprocal causality among three influence processes: personal, behavioural, and environmental (Bandura, 1986; Zimmerman, 1989).

Based on this view of self-regulated learning, a structured interview for assessing student use of self-regulated learning strategies was developed (Zimmerman & Martinez-Pons, 1986). The Self-Regulated Learning Interview Schedule (SRLIS) has been used to correlate student strategy use with academic achievement (Zimmerman & Martinez-Pons, 1986); with teacher ratings of students' use of self-regulatory strategies, and students' verbal achievement (Zimmerman & Martinez-Pons, 1988); and with student perceptions of both verbal and mathematical efficacy (Zimmerman & Martinez-Pons, 1990). It is planned to use a form of the SRLIS, modified to cater for cross-cultural differences in an educational context, to assess the strategy use of subjects in the proposed research project.

Conceptions of learning

Students' conceptions of learning have been found to be one component of the skill of self-regulated learning (Säljö, 1979). According to Säljö, when students perceive learning to be a reproductive process, the responsibility for transmitting an already existing body of knowledge into the head of the learner lies with an external source. In contrast, however, when learning is viewed as a meaning-centred process, the learner is more likely to assume responsibility for construing knowledge by proactively initiating and regulating the (re)construction process.

Six distinctly different conceptions of learning have been identified in research (Marton, Dall'Alba, & Beatty, 1993; Säljö, 1979). These six different conceptions (increasing one's knowledge, memorizing and reproducing, applying, understanding, seeing something in a different way, and changing as a person) have been used in research to demonstrate that students from different cultures do conceive of learning in different ways (Marton, 1992; Watkins & Regmi, 1992). There are two aspects to a person's conception of learning: a way of seeing *what* is learned and a way of seeing *how* it is learned (Marton, Dall'Alba & Beatty, 1993). The implications for self-regulation learning theory with regard to the *how* of learning are clear. *How* a student perceives learning to occur will determine the set of strategies selected to achieve the desired outcome.

There is some evidence to suggest that students from different cultures do understand learning in different ways (Watkins & Regmi, 1992). If this is so for students from south-east Asian countries who are being schooled in Australia, then there are obvious implications for teachers and the classroom practices adopted by them.

Second language competence and self-regulated learning

Research findings that verbal achievement and verbal efficacy are correlated significantly with strategy use (Zimmerman & Martinez-Pons, 1988, 1990) are particularly pertinent to this proposed study. It is hypothesized that second language users, who are not yet fully competent in their second language, will be disadvantaged in their use of self-regulated strategies because of assumed weaknesses in verbal ability and verbal efficacy. Of the 14 strategies identified by Zimmerman and Martinez-Pons (1986), over half (self-evaluation, organizing and transforming, seeking information, keeping records and monitoring, rehearsing and memorizing, seeking social assistance – from peers, teachers, and adults, reviewing records – tests, notes and textbooks) require students to use one or more of the macro-skills of speaking, listening, reading and writing in the target language. Depending on the level of development in these four skills, students will be variously disadvantaged in their attempts to employ strategies that require direct use of one or more of the macro-skills in their second language.

The interaction between language proficiency and the use of self-regulated learning strategies is further complicated by the verbalizations or private speech of students. Such speech is directed towards the self in order to facilitate the execution of a task. It has been shown to improve coding, storage, and retention of information thereby aiding the process of future retrieval and use (Denney, 1975; Schunk, 1986); verbalization can improve students' self-efficacy for performing tasks (Schunk, 1986) which in turn can promote task motivation and learning (Schunk, 1985); by using self-reinforcement and coping verbalizations, students may be better able to maintain a positive task orientation and cope with difficulties (Michenbaum & Asarnow, 1979). These findings all point to the key role of verbalization in developing self-regulated learning in students.

Another potential problem for second language users lies in the area of the use of the social strategies of self-regulated learning (i.e. seeking assistance from peers, teachers, and other adults). In this respect, not only is there the problem of limited oral proficiency which could well discourage students from attempting to use these strategies but there is also the possibility of conflict arising out of different cultural and educational backgrounds. For some second language users, it is perceived to be inappropriate behaviour to seek personal assistance from the teacher. Furthermore, even though the seeking of assistance from peers may be viewed as acceptable behaviour by second language users, and is a previously highly practised activity for some (Tang, 1990), lack of confidence in their ability to approach peers successfully, to be clearly understood and to correctly understand their responses may be too strong a deterrent to the use of this strategy.

Finally, there is some research that suggests that studying in a second language will influence a student's approach to learning (Watkins, Biggs & Regmi, 1991). Students less confident in a second language tend to rely more on rote learning whereas those with greater confidence are low on surface and high on deep approaches to learning. This suggests that an increase in second language competence will be associated with an increased ability to employ self-regulated learning strategies in the execution of academic tasks.

(v) Research questions

1. What self-regulated learning strategies are used by Asian students in their native educational settings?

2. Do the self-regulated learning strategies of Asian students change when they become learners in Australian schools, using English as a second language? If so, in what ways?
3. What do Asian students actually understand by the term 'learning'?
4. Do the conceptions of learning held by Asian students change when they become students in Australian schools?
5. What is the relationship between students' conceptions of learning and their use of self-regulated learning strategies?
6. What, if any, are the differences between the conceptions of learning and the use of self-regulated learning strategies of Asian and Australian students?
7. Does the level of English language competence of Asian students in Australian schools affect their use of self-regulated learning strategies?

B. Research Plan

(i) Methods and approaches

Study 1

Purpose The purpose of this study is to design an interview schedule that is appropriate for use with both Australian secondary school students and students from two different Asian countries. In order for an interview schedule to provide reliable and valid information, a number of factors need to be kept in mind. Segall (1986) noted the following as important considerations in the construction of a cross-cultural interview schedule: efficiency with relation to time and cost; the construction of a set of questions which serve a purpose, which are unambiguous, which allow the interviewer to insert probe questions to obtain more elaboration of answers already given, and which make it easy for the respondent to answer; the use of translation techniques that will maximize correct interpretation of responses; and the development of appropriate coding and scoring systems.

Using the above guidelines for the construction of a reliable and valid instrument, an interview schedule, based on that developed by Zimmerman and Martinez-Pons (1986, 1990), will be designed. This interview schedule will assess 14 categories of self-regulated learning strategies (self-evaluation; organizing and transforming; goal-setting and planning; seeking information; keeping records and monitoring; environmental structuring; self-consequences; rehearsing and memorizing; seeking peer, teacher or adult assistance; reviewing tests, notes, and texts; and other).

A number of different learning contexts will be identified both from the Zimmerman & Martinez-Pons studies and from pilot interviews with newly arrived Asian students and students who are accustomed to the Australian secondary school learning environment. This will ensure that learning contexts will be valid for all participants taking part in this research. The following is an example of a learning context that could be described:

> Imagine your teacher is discussing with your class the influence of twentieth century developments in technology on the lives of people today. Your teacher says that you will be tested on the topic the next day. Do you have a method that you would use to help you learn and remember the information being discussed? What if you are having trouble understanding or remembering the information discussed in class?
>
> (Adapted from Zimmerman & Martinez-Pons, 1990)

Zimmerman and Martinez-Pons (1986) described procedures for the coding of protocols which resulted in an interrater agreement level of 86%. Three different scoring procedures – strategy use, strategy frequency and strategy consistency – were developed to summarize the categorical data obtained. A pilot study using a small group of students from Perth metropolitan schools will be used to check the appropriateness of these procedures and refine them where possible. This group of students will include representatives of the three types of students used for this research and who are described in the following two studies.

Study 2

Purpose   This study will investigate conceptions of learning and the use of self-regulated learning strategies of Asian students from two different countries before they have been exposed to schooling in Australia.

Participants   The participants will be 60 newly arrived Asian students who are about to commence an intensive English language programme prior to entry into upper secondary (Years 11 and 12) education in Perth. Costs associated with the translation of interview data make it impossible to include students from a large number of Asian countries. Students from two Asian countries will be selected from Perth schools, depending on availability at the time of the study. In order to ensure that responses to questions in the interview schedule are based on the learning strategies students have developed for use in their native learning environments rather than strategies that have been influenced by exposure to other learning environments, it is important that students have not had previous schooling in a non-native learning environment.

Procedures   The self-regulated learning interview schedule developed in Study 1 will be presented separately to each student in his or her native language by trained interviewers. The interviewers will have been acquainted with the nature and purpose of the study and trained to present the interview schedule in such a way as to elicit from students answers that are as fully elaborated as possible. A number of different learning contexts will be described to students and they will be asked to indicate the methods they would normally use in the situations described.

Students will also be asked to respond to the question 'What do you actually understand by learning?'.

Student responses to questions will be recorded by the interviewer, who will later translate these into English. All interviews will be tape-recorded to enable subsequent checking of responses.

Data analysis   Coding and scoring procedures developed in Study 1 will be applied to student responses to the self-regulated learning interview schedule.

Using methodology described by Marton and Säljö (1984), responses to the question about conceptions of learning will be analysed and coded according to the six levels: increasing one's knowledge; memorizing and reproducing; applying; understanding; seeing something in a different way; and changing as a person. Briefly, this approach to the analysis of the transcripts will involve the identification and grouping, on the basis of similarities, differences and complementarities, students' responses to the question 'What do you actually understand by learning?'

Multiple regression analyses will be used to determine if there is an association between learning strategy use and conceptions of learning. For instance, do students who use more self-regulated learning strategies tend to understand learning more in the last three ways as opposed to the first three ways?

Study 3

Purpose The purpose of this study is to investigate the use of self-regulated learning strategies by two groups of secondary school students: native speakers of English; and Asian students whose second language is English, who have been studying in Australian schools for at least two years, and who have achieved at least an intermediate level of competence in the use of English. Patterns of strategy use of these two groups and the group of students from the second study will be compared in order to establish if differences exist between the groups.

The study will also investigate the conceptions of learning held by the native speakers of English and the Asian students. These will be compared with the conceptions of students in the first study.

Finally, the study will investigate the relationship between the two levels of English language proficiency (intermediate and advanced) and the patterns of self-regulated learning strategy use of the Asian students.

Participants Ninety Year 12 students studying at Perth metropolitan high schools will be used for this study. Thirty will be native speakers of English and 60 will be non-native English speakers from similar Asian language backgrounds to those in the second study. They will have been studying in Australian schools for at least two years. Half of the non-English speaking background students will be at an 'intermediate' level of language proficiency and half will be at an 'advanced' level. Students will be assigned to proficiency groups according to language test scores and on teacher recommendation.

Procedure The question 'What exactly do you understand by learning?' and the self-regulated learning interview schedule will be presented (in English) to students in a similar manner to that used in Study 2. Depending on information gained from Study 2 with respect to the category 'other', further categories of strategy will be added to the existing 13, or, if no new strategies did emerge, this category will remain as 'other'.

Data analysis Responses to the strategy interview schedule and the question about conceptions of learning will be coded and scored as for Study 2. As the data will be frequency counts, log linear analysis will be used to assess differences in strategy use and conceptions of learning across the four groups.

What efforts have been made to ensure that the project does not duplicate work already done?

An extensive search of the literature has been undertaken since February, 1993. Searches on ERIC and Psychlit, and an examination of recent editions of CIJE and bibliographies obtained from key journal articles has produced a large collection of readings related to self-regulated learning and conceptions of learning. Although these two areas have been well researched, a cross-cultural perspective has not been applied. Furthermore, the two areas have been researched independently of each other and no evidence of linking theory and findings in the manner proposed in this research has been found.

Confidentiality

All information pertaining to participants will remain the property of the researcher and will not be used for any purpose except for execution of this study. Students' names will not be used other than for organization of the raw data.

[b] QUALITATIVE PROPOSAL

Name of Candidate: Ron Chalmers

Degree: Doctor of Philosophy, The University of Western Australia

A. Proposed Study

(i) Title

The inclusion of children with a severe or profound intellectual disability in regular classrooms: how teachers manage the situation.

(ii) The research aim

The aim of this study is to use grounded theory methods to develop a theory about how primary school teachers in rural schools in Western Australia manage the situation of having a child with a severe or profound intellectual disability included in their classroom during the course of one school year.

Currently, in Western Australia, children with intellectual disabilities are taught in a variety of educational settings by teachers from a wide range of backgrounds. The vast majority of children with a severe or profound intellectual disability attend education support schools, centres or units. In rural and remote areas of the state where education support facilities do not exist, a relatively small number of children with this level of disability (35 primary school students in 1994) attend their local school and are included in a regular classroom. This study will focus on regular classroom teachers in country schools who are called upon to include a child with a severe or profound intellectual disability in their class.

The study will be limited to primary school teachers because, unlike their secondary school colleagues, they have the responsibility for the total educational programme and the duty of care for their class of students throughout the school day. Inclusion in secondary schools typically involves numerous teachers and a variety of classroom settings. Furthermore, the number of children with a severe or profound intellectual disability who are currently included in the regular class-rooms of secondary schools is extremely small.

The study will use the criteria set by the Education Department of Western Australia to define severe and profound intellectual disability. The Department, utilizing the criteria for determining levels of severity developed by the Australian Council of Education Research, estimates that 0.1% of the population have a severe disability, and 0.05% of the population have a profound disability. A severely disabled child is described as having 'an IQ in the range 25 to 39, minimal speech and poor motor development, an inability to learn functional academic skills, and a capacity to profit from systematic habit-training' (de Lemos, 1993, p. 22). A profoundly disabled child is described as having 'an IQ below 24, minimal capacity for functioning, some motor or speech development, and a requirement of complete care and supervision' (de Lemos, 1993, p. 22).

In this proposal, the terms inclusive education and inclusion will be used deliberately in preference to the term integration. Inclusion will refer to situations in which a student with a disability is 'embedded within the normative educative pathways within the classroom and school' (Uditsky, 1993, p. 88), and in which the regular classroom teacher is responsible for the student's education. In contrast, in the Western Australia education system, the term integration is used to describe situations in which children with disabilities are located in education support units or centres, are the responsibility of education support teachers, and spend only parts of the school day in regular classrooms. In the wider education community the term integration has been used to describe many different types of placement. Terms such as physical integration, systematic integration, reciprocal integration, and associative integration are used to describe particular strategies for increasing the level of interaction between children with disabilities and their non-disabled peers. Each one of these forms of integration is something other than inclusive education as defined for this study.

(iii) The research context

The move towards the integration and inclusion of children with intellectual disabilities into mainstream education has been a feature of Western education systems for the past 15 years. This development has been largely the result of 'intensive advocacy for integration of people with disabilities into all areas of community life' (Sobsey & Dreimanis, 1993, p. 1).

Integrated or inclusive education contrasts markedly with the response of Western societies to the education of children with disabilities in earlier decades. At the turn of the century the vast majority of children with intellectual disabilities were considered ineducable and subsequently excluded from any form of formal education (Galloway, 1985; Uditsky, 1993). In many countries there was no distinction made between children with intellectual disabilities and people with mental disorders. At the end of World War II, special education became a feature of public education in many countries (Barton & Tomlinson, 1986; Booth, 1981). Children with disabilities began to gain access to formal education, but only within the confines of special education systems.

The pressure for inclusion has come primarily from the parents of children with disabilities, educators and other community advocates (National Institute on Mental Retardation, 1981; Stainback, Stainback & Bunch, 1989). These groups have used powerful moral, social and political arguments in support of their case. One of the most persuasive arguments is that all children gain through inclusion. Studies indicate that, given proper guidance, students can learn in inclusive settings to understand, respect, be sensitive to, and grow comfortable with the individual differences and similarities amongst their peers (McHale & Simeonsson, 1980; Voeltz, 1980, p. 182). Stainback and Stainback (1985) observe that:

> . . . there are many nonhandicapped persons who realise a tremendous range of emotional and social benefits from their involvements with persons who experience severe handicaps.

Advocates for inclusion also contend that segregated education leads to segregation in adult life, and that inclusion in education has the opposite effect. The assertion here is that positive attitudes toward people with disabilities are developed when disabled and non-disabled children interact at school, and that these attitudes are sustained in adult life (see, for example, Bricker, 1978; Snyder, Apolloni, & Cooke, 1977).

Inclusion in education has also been portrayed as a human rights issue. The arguments used to enhance the participation rates of racial minorities and females in education have been used as the basis for promoting the inclusion of children with disabilities in schools. The landmark Victorian Report of the Ministerial Review of Educational Services for the Disabled (Collins, 1984), proposed that the development of policy be underpinned by five guiding principles. Significantly, the first principle was that every child has a right to be educated in an ordinary classroom in a regular class.

A number of commentators, including Bilken (1985) and Keogh (1990) have observed that the strength of the inclusive education movement has come from the values that underpin the cause rather than from the findings of studies into the outcomes of inclusion. According to Conway (1991), the introduction of policies intended to encourage inclusion has occurred not as an outcome of empirical research but as a result of changes in public attitudes about the way the wider community responds to people with disabilities.

It should not be inferred from this that there has been a dearth of research into aspects of inclusive education. The research literature in this field of education is extensive. The vast majority of this research has been characterized by the application of traditional quantitative methodologies. Experiments and questionnaire surveys in large-N studies have been the norm. The findings from quantitative research conducted during the past 15 years have contributed significantly to the field of special education and, more specifically, to the segregation–inclusion debate. Curriculum design, resourcing teacher training, administrative arrangements and efficacy research have been favoured areas for investigation.

There are, however, increasing calls for more qualitative research in this field of education (Biklen & Moeley, 1988; Hegarty and Evans, 1989; Patton, 1990; Salisbury, Palombaro & Hollowood, 1993; Stainback & Stainback, 1989). Hegarty (1989, p. 110) stated that there are 'many topics in special education that are best explored by means of qualitative methods of inquiry'. These include investigations into pupils' and teachers' perspectives and experiences of particular education programmes; clarifying the implications of various policy options; evaluating innovations; and providing detailed accounts of various forms of special education provision.

Despite these calls, Vulliamy and Webb (1993, p. 190) observed that:

> There have been relatively few published qualitative research studies on the theme of special education, despite the prominent impact of qualitative research on educational research more generally.

More research of this kind is needed to gain a greater understanding of the phenomenon of inclusive education from the perspectives of the people involved (teachers, parents, school administrators and students) in their natural settings. We need 'in-depth, penetrating investigation that strives for relational understanding of all the various factors that comprise and affect the object of the . . . study' (Wolf, 1979, p. 5). The development of theories about inclusion, grounded in data gathered from teachers and other school-based personnel contribute significantly to this field of education, inform teachers who find themselves in similar situations in the future, and guide the development of policy for the education of students with disabilities.

There are clear indications that an increasing number of Australian children with intellectual disabilities will be educated in regular classrooms (see DEET, 1993; Education Department of Western Australia, 1992) and, correspondingly, that an increasing number of Western Australian primary school teachers will experience the phenomenon of inclusive education. Given that the outcomes of inclusion initiatives depend on the beliefs, values and attitudes of teachers (Cohen & Cohen, 1986), in the Western Australian context there needs to be a greater understanding of what teachers think and believe about this phenomenon, and how these thoughts and beliefs change over time.

(iii) This study's substantial and original contribution to knowledge

The aim of this study is to use grounded theory methods to build theory about a specific aspect of education where no theory currently exists. To date there is very little knowledge and no explanatory theory about the way primary school teachers in rural and remote schools manage inclusion. An extensive search of the research literature has failed to identify studies that have examined this particular phenomenon. The theory that will be generated from this study will be an original contribution to the knowledge base of the emerging field of inclusive education.

The importance of inclusive education in the 1990s

A number of recent developments indicate that the education of students with disabilities is one of the most important issues facing the Western Australian school system. In December 1992 the then Ministry of Education established the Task Force on the Education of Students with Disabilities and Specific Learning Difficulties in response to 'growing parent concerns about the problems faced by children with disabilities' (Ministerial Task Force, 1993, p. v). The Task Force report listed sixty recommendations to government. Many of these recommendations relate specifically to the role of the teacher in educating students with disabilities. In February 1994 the Minister for Education responded to the report. The Minister announced that the education of students with disabilities and specific learning difficulties would be a priority for the next three years and that schools will be required to reflect this in their school development plans. Additional resources ($6 million over the next triennium) will be allocated to implement recommendations in the Task Force report.

A recent Commonwealth Government report entitled Project of National Significance: Students with Disabilities in Regular Classrooms (1993), reinforces the importance for school systems and educational researchers of examining the role of the teacher in the inclusion of children with disabilities. The study outlined in this present proposal is therefore both relevant and timely. The findings will make a significant contribution to the understanding of an aspect of education that has become a priority in the current decade.

Research into aspects of inclusive education in Western Australia

The limited research conducted in Western Australia into aspects of inclusive education has tended to focus on children with mild to moderate intellectual disability (see, for example, Bain & Dolbel, 1991; Roberts & Naylor, 1994; Roberts & Zubrick, 1992). The inclusion of students with severe or profound disability has not attracted the attention of the local research community. This trend is consistent with the research focus in other education systems and in other nations. Within the context of the Western Australian education system this study will break new ground because it will focus exclusively on situations where the most disabled students are being included in regular classrooms.

The descriptors used by the Western Australian Education Department to categorize a child as severely or profoundly intellectually disabled are significantly different to the descriptors used to categorize a child as mildly or moderately intellectually disabled. Findings from the relatively substantial amount of research conducted into aspects of inclusive education for children with mild to moderate disabilities may not be relevant for an understanding of inclusion for students with more severe disability who present with a range of different functional characteristics. The findings from this study will go some way towards addressing this imbalance in the research focus.

The use of grounded theory

A preliminary examination of the research literature has failed to identify research studies that have used grounded theory methods to examine the way teachers manage the situation of having a child with a disability included in their class. This study is therefore uniquely placed to generate theory, grounded in data collected from rural schools in Western Australia, about this particular phenomenon.

It is anticipated that the theory that emerges from this study will be comprehensible and make sense to those teachers who will be studied. Also, the nature of grounded theory is such that the emergent theory 'will be abstract enough and include sufficient variation to make it applicable to a variety of contexts related to that phenomenon' (Strauss & Corbin, 1990, p. 23). In other words, the theory developed from this research will be of use to other teachers involved with inclusion, as well as other groups such as school administrators, educational policy makers, and members of the wider educational research community.

Grounded theory has been used extensively as a research methodology in sociology, and in nursing and related fields. It has been used less widely in education. This study will provide an opportunity for observations to be made about the applicability of this mode of research in education, and more specifically in the field of inclusive education.

B. The Research Plan

(i) The research questions

The central question of this research is as follows:

> *How do primary school teachers manage the situation of having a child with a severe or profound intellectual disability included in their classroom for a period of one year?*

The study, and especially the data-gathering process, will be guided by the following eight questions:

1. What are teachers' expectations of what is going to be involved when they realize they will have a child with a severe or profound intellectual disability in their class for the year, and what philosophical standpoint do they have about inclusion?
2. What are teachers' perceptions of the expectations of the school principal, other teachers and parents of them regarding their management of the inclusion situation? How do these perceptions change over the course of the year?
3. How does the teacher organize the classroom and education programme to accommodate the child with the severe or profound intellectual disability, and how does this change over the course of the year?
4. What are the characteristics of the relationship between the teacher and the rest of the children in the class, and how does this relationship develop over the course of the year?
5. What are the characteristics of the relationship between the teacher and the rest of the school staff, and how does this relationship develop over the course of the year?
6. How does the teacher manage the interaction between the child with the severe or profound intellectual disability and other students in the class?
7. What are the characteristics of the relationship between the teacher and the parents of the child with a severe or profound intellectual disability, and how does this relationship develop during the year?

8. What relationships develop between the teacher and the parents of non-disabled children in the class? What are the characteristics of these relationships and how do they change over the course of the year?

(ii) The research method

Research design

This study will use grounded theory methodology. Grounded theory is a research method that offers a comprehensive and systematic framework for inductively building theory. A grounded theory is one that is discovered, developed, and provisionally verified through systematic data collection and analysis of data pertaining to a particular phenomenon (Strauss & Corbin, 1990). The careful and precise application of this method will ensure that the theory to emerge from this study will meet the criteria of good science; generalizability, reproducibility, precision, rigour, and verification (Corbin & Strauss, 1990).

A number of the basic features of grounded theory make it an appropriate method for this research. These include:

1. Grounded theory methodology specifically includes analysis of process. Within grounded theory methodology the term process is used to describe 'the linking of sequences of action/interaction as they pertain to the management of, control over, or response to, a phenomenon' (Strauss & Corbin, 1990, p. 143). Process is the analyst's way of accounting for or explaining change. An important aspect of this research will be to monitor the way teachers manage inclusion over the entire school year. The research questions have been constructed to guide data collection and analysis in ways that will highlight and account for any changes in teacher management as well as the ways teachers manage changing conditions that may occur during the year. In this way process will be analysed both as progressive movement characterized by phases or stages, and as 'non-progressive movement, that is as purposeful alterations or changes in action/interaction in response to changes in conditions' (Strauss & Corbin, 1990, p. 52). The first conceptualization of process will involve an analysis of the conditions and corresponding actions that move the teacher from one phase or stage of management to another. The conceptualization of process as non-progressive will involve analysis of the adjustments taken by teachers in response to changing conditions throughout the year.
2. Grounded theory methodology directly links macroscopic issues to the phenomenon under investigation. This mode of research requires that broader, contextual issues, that are shown to influence the phenomenon under study, be given appropriate recognition in the development of theory. Rather than focusing the investigation by disregarding these broader conditions, every effort will be made to acknowledge and account for them.
3. Grounded theory makes its greatest contribution in areas in which little research has been done. As stated previously, little research has been conducted specifically into aspects of the management of the inclusion of children with severe or profound intellectual disabilities in regular classrooms. Most of the research in this field has tended to focus on chidlren with mild to moderate disabilities (for example, Center & Curry, 1993; Chambers & Kay, 1992; Deno, Maruyama, Espin & Cohen, 1990; Roberts & Zubrick, 1992), and on integration, mainstreaming, or some other form of placement that differs from inclusion (for example, Biklen, 1985; Center, et al., 1988; Taylor, 1988). The paucity of research about inclusion means that many of the variables

relevant to the concepts of this phenomenon are yet to be identified. Grounded theory is an appropriate methodology for this study as it will generate theory that can be used as a precursor for further investigation of this phenomenon and related issues. Other qualitative research techniques, quantitative methods, or a combination of both, can then be used in subsequent studies to test, verify or extend the qualitative hypotheses that emerge from this initial research.

The study population

The population for this study will be all primary school teachers in Western Australian country schools who, in the 1995 school year, have a child with a severe or profound intellectual disability included in their class. Information provided by the Social Justice Branch of the Education Department of Western Australia indicates that in 1994 there are 25 Government school teachers in this situation. It is anticipated that in 1995 this number will increase to approximately 28. Within the non-Government school systems (Catholic Education Commission and the Association of Independent Schools) there are approximately 10 teachers in this situation in the current year. This number is not expected to increase in 1995. It is therefore estimated that the total population for this study will be 38 teachers.

The study sample

It is estimated that approximately 25 of the 38 teachers in the study population will be in school districts in the southern half of Western Australia. For logistical reasons the gathering of data for this study will be restricted to these southern districts (Esperance, Albany, Manjimup, Bunbury North, Bunbury South, Narrogin, Peel, Northam and Merredin). Of the 25 teachers that remain as candidates for this study, it is likely that a small proportion are unlikely to accept the invitation to become involved. This leaves a field of approximately 20 teachers.

Six teachers will be selected, at random, to provide the first body of data. This will be the initial sample group. Subsequent data collection will be guided by the theoretical sampling principle of grounded theory. Where necessary, data will be gathered from all 20 teachers if theoretical saturation on any particular category has not been achieved at an earlier stage.

In this study other decisions about the sampling process will be made during the research process itself. In a grounded theory study theoretical sampling cannot be fully planned before the study commences.

Data collection

In this study data-gathering methods will include semi-structured interviews, teacher diaries, observations, and document analysis. Data will be gathered from the initial sample group in a cyclical process as outlined in the timetable below.

- Semi-structured interviews (round 1), December 1994 – January 1995
- Teacher diary entries (5 days), term 1, 1995
- Semi-structured interviews (round 2), end of term 1, 1995
- Observations of teachers; 2 days per teacher (round 1), early term 2, 1995
- Teacher diary entries (5 days) early term 3, 1995
- Semi-structured interviews (round 3), early term 3, 1995
- Observations of teachers; 2 days per teacher (round 2), term 3, 1995
- Teacher diary entries (5 days), term 4, 1994
- Semi-structured interviews (round 4), term 4, 1995.

This timetable is a tentative plan for data gathering. In grounded theory studies data gathering and analysis are tightly interwoven processes; data analysis guides future data collection. Therefore, changes may be made to this provisional timetable if the analysis of data collected early in the school year indicates a need to adopt a different sequence of data-gathering processes.

The precise timing of interviews, diary entries and observations will also depend on events in individual schools. It may be possible to anticipate, at the start of the school year, crucial events or periods in the school calendar that are likely to influence the way the teacher responds to the phenomenon of inclusion. These may include the first parents' meeting, the annual swimming carnival, or the first class excursion. As far as possible, data-gathering activities will be timed to coincide with, or immediately follow, these school events.

Semi-structured interviews will be used as the primary means of data collection. Initially, arrangements will be made to interview each of the teachers in the initial study sample on four occasions during the course of the school year. These interviews will be tape recorded. The first round of interviews will be structured to gather data about the widest possible range of issues associated with the phenomenon under study. The research questions will guide the data-gathering process. The structure and content of subsequent interviews will be determined after the data analysis process has commenced. The second, third and fourth rounds of interviews will be used to (a) gather new data about known concepts and categories that will have been developed about the phenomenon, (b) gather new data about the phenomenon, and (c) involve the teachers in a process of testing and verifying data and the emerging theory.

Each of the teachers included in the initial study sample will be requested to maintain a tape recorded diary for three periods during the year. On each of these occasions, the teacher will be encouraged to make entries into a handheld micro tape recorder for a period of five days (one school week). Every effort will be made to ensure that the teacher is comfortable with the tape diary technique and that they are clear about the purposes of this data-gathering procedure.

Tape diaries serve a number of purposes (Burgess, 1984, p. 203). Firstly, these diaries provide first-hand accounts of situations to which the researcher may not have direct access. Secondly, they provide 'insiders' accounts of situations. Finally, they provide further sampling of informants, of activities and of time which may complement the observations made by the researcher.

In this study, diary entries will (a) provide the researcher with information about critical incidents that relate to the phenomenon under investigation, (b) serve as a record of the teachers' perceptions of their experiences with inclusion, (c) act as a triangulation strategy, and (d) stimulate and direct the data-gathering process in subsequent interview sessions. The value of the link between the analysis of diary data and subsequent interviews is highlighted by Burgess (1984, p. 203) when he states that:

> . . . in cases where the researcher obtains an informant's diary, it may be scanned for data that needs to be elaborated, discussed, explored and illustrated, all of which are tasks that can be conducted in an interview.

Teachers will be encouraged to keep the tape recorder with them (at home, in the car, as well as at school) throughout the five days to record as much information as possible about their experiences in managing inclusion. They will be given a brief overview of critical incident technique and encouraged to report critical incidents. They will also be advised to record their thoughts, feelings, beliefs and attitudes about these critical incidents and about the management of inclusion generally. It is anticipated that the data from each of the interviews will highlight categories that will provide a degree of focus for teachers in the use of their tape diaries.

The decision to limit the periods of diary keeping to five days is based on the experiences of other researchers who have used diary techniques (see Sommer & Sommer, 1986). The primary objective is to gather the maximum amount of relevant data without the process becoming tedious for the teacher.

The third major data-gathering technique will be observation. Direct observation of how individual teachers manage the inclusion of a child with a severe or profound intellectual disability will provide the data required to verify and corroborate the information gained through interviews and diary entries. It will also allow the researcher to find cases in which there is a mismatch between interview data and teacher behaviour; where teachers do not do or act as they say they do. This will ensure that the theory generated from this research is based on more than the perceptions of teachers. School-based observations will also allow the researcher to pursue and test out relationships between theoretically relevant categories.

Initially it is planned to conduct two rounds of observations of each teacher. Once again, this may change during the course of the year depending upon the categories that emerge. Similarly, decisions about matters such as participant versus non-participant observation, timing of observations, length of observations, questioning during observation, and data recording methods will be made on a site-by-site basis.

Data will be obtained from document analysis and interviews with other members of the school communities. Arrangements will be made to interview other members of the school staff at times throughout the year. It is not possible, prior to the commencement of the data-gathering process, to predict the timing of these interviews or the actual staff members to be interviewed. Education Department and school documents will also be used as sources of data. It is anticipated that such documents will provide a 'rich source of information, contextually relevant and grounded in the contexts they represent' (Lincoln & Guba, 1985, p. 277).

A piloting exercise will be conducted during the fourth term of the 1994 school year. A teacher with a severe or profoundly intellectually disabled child included in their class in 1994 will be invited to (a) trial the teacher diary for one week, (b) respond to, and comment on, the draft interview schedule for the first round of semi-structured interviews, and (c) comment on their experiences with inclusion during the previous three terms. This process will fine tune the data-gathering methods and heighten my theoretical sensitivity towards the phenomenon of integration. Theoretical sensitivity refers to the 'attribute of having insight, the ability to give meaning to data, the capacity to understand, and capability to separate the pertinent from that which isn't' (Strauss & Corbin, 1990, p. 42).

Analysis of the data

Analysing data by the grounded theory method is an intricate process of reducing raw data into concepts that are designated to stand for categories. The categories are then developed and integrated into a theory (Corbin, 1986). This process is achieved by coding data, writing memos, and diagramming.

In this study, data will be coded and analysed using the three coding methods of the grounded theory model: open coding, axial coding and selective coding. Open coding is the process of breaking down, examining, comparing, conceptualizing, and categorizing data. The aim of open coding is the development of categories. Axial coding involves re-building the data (fractured through open coding) in new ways by establishing relationships between categories, and between categories and their sub-categories. Selective coding involves selecting a core category, systematically relating it to other categories, validating those relationships, and filling in categories that need further development or refinement.

It is through this process that all the interpretive work done over the course of the research is integrated to form a grounded theory.

Coding procedures, memo writing and diagramming will be used as data analysis strategies. Facts or incidents obtained from interviews, documents, or diary entries, will be coded in a systematic way. Memos will be written as records of analysis, and diagrams will be developed as visual representations of the relationships between concepts. Code notes, memos and diagrams will become progressively more detailed and sophisticated as the analysis moves through the three types of coding.

Throughout the data analysis process, the teachers and other participants in the research will be involved directly in verifying the data and the emerging theory.

Efforts made to ensure that the project does not duplicate work already done

During the past six months I have conducted an extensive review of the literature in the areas of special education, integration, and inclusive education. I have been unable to locate any research that utilizes grounded theory methodology to develop a theory about how primary school teachers manage the inclusion of children with severe or profound intellectual disabilities in their regular classroom.

Confidentiality

The informed consent of the following people will be obtained to the commencement of the study:

1. the principals of the nominated schools
2. the appropriate officers from the Catholic Education Commission and the Association of Independent Schools
3. the teachers chosen in the initial sample group
4. the parents of the children with disabilities.

The informed consent of other teachers and parents (chosen in the wider sample group) will be sought at the time they are approached to participate in the study.

All data will be treated in a way that protects the confidentiality and anonymity of the teachers, parents and children involved in the study. Coding will be used during the gathering and processing of interview notes, tapes and transcripts.

As noted earlier, the sections on Timetable, Scholars, Facilities, Estimated Costs and References, which are required in doctoral proposals at the University of Western Australia, are omitted from these proposals in this book, for space reasons.

Other proposals in the literature

Four 'specimen proposals' are included in the book by Locke et al. (1993: 185–296). There is extensive and helpful editorial comment on each, and they cover a range of research approaches. The four proposals are:

- 'The effects of age, modality, complexity of response and practice on reaction time' (experimental design);

- 'Returning women students in the community college' (qualitative study);
- 'Teaching children to question what they read: an attempt to improve reading comprehension through training in a cognitive learning strategy' (quasi-experimental design);
- 'A competition strategy for worksite smoking cessation' (funded grant).

Brink and Wood (1994: 255–375) include four sample research proposals, without editorial comment. The first two are descriptive studies, the third is a correlational study, and the fourth an experimental study. They are:

- 'Value orientations of Hutterian women in Canada';
- 'Eating patterns successful dieters use to maintain weight loss';
- 'The relationship between preterm infant sleep state disorganisation and maternal–infant interaction';
- 'Patient controlled analgesia for total hip arthroplasty patients'.

Madsen (1983: 109–54) has two sample proposals, the first historical, the second experimental. They are:

- 'The Carnegie Institute of Washington, 1901–1904: Andrew Carnegie, Daniel Gilman and John Billings search for the exceptional man';
- 'An investigation of two methods of achieving compliance with the severely handicapped in a classroom setting'.

Maxwell (1996: 116–37) reproduces, with commentary, a qualitative proposal entitled 'How basic science teachers help medical students learn: the students' perspective'.

Maykut and Morehouse (1994: 165–77) include two shorter qualitative proposals, one on school climate, the other entitled 'An exploration of how children and adolescents with autism or autistic tendencies use facilitated communication in their lives'.

Coley and Scheinberg (1990: 112–24) give the example, with critique, of a proposal for an intervention project where a community wants to address the problem of unintended adolescent pregnancy.

Similarly, the proposal for an intervention project entitled 'A program to train interdisciplinary health care teams to work with the homeless' is presented and critiqued, as a case study, by Gitlin and Lyons (1996: 195–203).

Gilpatrick (1989) gives a progressive commentary and critique, throughout her book, of five intervention projects in a funding context. They are:

- 'Education for parents of infants discharged from intensive care';
- 'Ambulance staff training in emergency medical services';
- 'City children involved in the arts community';
- 'Writing skills for retention of graduate students';
- 'Development of leadership by women of color in the antiviolence movement'.

Wallen and Fraenkel (1991: 267–87) critique two student research proposals in education. They are: 'The effects of individualized reading upon student motivation in grade four' and 'The effects of a peer-counselling class on self esteem'.

Finally, O'Donoghue and Haynes (1997: 91–169) give six examples of proposals in education, with these titles:

- 'Goal directed behaviour, reputation enhancement and juvenile delinquency';
- 'The inclusion of children with a severe or profound intellectual disability in regular classrooms: how teachers manage the situation';
- 'Teacher of all the Gods: The educational thought of Ki Hajar Dewantara';
- 'An analysis of emergence, development and implementation of Italian as a school subject in the curriculum of Western Australian secondary schools over the period 1968 to 1994';
- 'Ideal algebra word problem test design: an application of the Rasch Model for Partial Credit Scoring';
- 'Language, thought and reality: a critical reassessment of the ideas of Benjamin Lee Whorf'.

NOTES

1 Despite this, some of the literature has diagrams and flow charts of steps and stages to go through in developing a proposal. For example, Locke et al. (1993: 54–5) suggest 20 steps to a proposal, Coley and Scheinberg (1990: 18–27) describe nine steps, and Hamper and Baugh (1996: 17–24) also have a nine-step proposal preparation process.

2 This means it is often frustrating in developing the proposal. That frustration is balanced by the satisfaction of achieving a convincing and acceptable finished proposal – especially one that is approved.

3 For the same reason I would also recommend finding out about the process of dissertation examination in your department, and consulting previous dissertations.

4 Personal experience, curiosity based on something in the media, the state of knowledge in a field, solving a problem (often associated with

professional experience), 'social premiums', personal values and everyday life.

5 Clinical or professional experience, professional literature, interaction with others, societal trends, legislative initiatives, public documents and agency goals and priorities.

6 For this reason, a term often used is 'ABD', which means 'all but the dissertation'.

7 Balancing these points, the writer needs to remember also that the proposal is an argument, and needs to be convincing and (within reason) confident. This is another tension which exists in the research planning process.

8 Or insights, or hunches, or relevant 'experiential data'.

9 For a short discussion and for direction to some of the literature on this topic, see *Introduction to Social Research* (Punch, 1988), Chapter 12, especially pp. 278–9 and pp. 282–4.

10 The sections omitted are Timetable, Scholars, Facilities and Estimated Costs.

Appendix 1: Disentangling the Terms 'Perspective', 'Strategy' and 'Design'

There is sometimes confusion with the terms 'perspectives', 'strategy' and 'design'. This appendix suggests a way of ordering these terms, while acknowledging some inevitable overlap between perspective and strategy, and between strategy and design.

In Chapter 4, I used *perspective* as a general term to refer to the paradigm, metatheory, or philosophical assumptions behind a piece of research. Examples of perspectives are positivism, postpositivism, critical theory, constructivism, feminism and postmodernism. The perspective may or may not be made explicit in the research proposal or project. The research may start from a perspective such as one of these, or it may start from the pragmatic position of questions needing answers.

Strategy can then be seen as something which is consistent with (or follows from) a perspective, which implements that perspective, and which, together with the perspective, leads to a set of research questions. In this sense, the strategy of the research is its internal logic or rationale – the set of ideas which will guide the study in answering its research questions (or testing its hypotheses). Both quantitative and qualitative approaches to research have a number of typical consistently used strategies.

Quantitative research strategies

The most common general strategies here are the experiment, the quasi experiment and the (correlational) survey. But there are others, most of which are more specialized. Examples are: normative surveys, longitudinal studies, time series analysis, panel studies, causal path studies, structural equation modelling, hierarchical linear modelling, event history analysis, facet design and analysis, Q methodology, cluster analysis, cohort analysis, mobility analysis, unidimensional scaling and multidimensional scaling, operations research and multiattribute evaluation.

Qualitative research strategies

Here, as usual, the situation is more diverse. Denzin and Lincoln (1994: 202–8) suggest the following eight main categories of qualitative strategy, noting that each has its own history and literature, its own exemplary works, and its own preferred ways for putting the strategy into motion: the case study, ethnography and participant observation, phenomenology, ethnomethodology and interpretive practice, grounded theory, the biographical method, the historical method, applied and action research, and clinical models.

Janesick (1994: 212) has this list of qualitative research strategies, noting that it is not meant to include all possibilities: ethnography, life history, oral history, ethnomethodology, case study, participant observation, field research or field study, naturalistic study, phenomenological study, ecological descriptive study, descriptive study, symbolic interactionist study, microethnography, interpretive research, action research, narrative research, historiography, and literary criticism.

Morse (1994: 224–5) has a slightly different list again: phenomenology, ethnography, grounded theory, ethnomethodology, discourse analysis and participant observation, qualitative ethology and ethnoscience.

These overlapping lists show the many different strategies possible in qualitative research. As a judgement about which of these seem most common, and with space limitations applying, *Introduction to Research* (Punch, 1988) concentrated on case studies, ethnography (including observation and participant observation) and grounded theory, but also gave some attention to the language-based strategies of narratives, ethnomethodology and conversation analysis, discourse analysis, semiotics, and documentary and textual analysis.

To move now from strategy to design, for both quantitative and qualitative research, *design* can be seen as something which implements the strategy. It deals with the general question 'Who or what will be studied, and how?' and begins with the strategy selected. Thus, as shown in Chapter 5, it can be broken down into these four more specific questions. The data will be collected (and analysed):

- Following what strategy?
- Within what framework?
- From whom?
- How?

Each of these questions is discussed in Chapter 5.

A benefit of this way of seeing these terms is that it suggests the components which need to fit together to ensure the overall validity of a piece of research. When all of them apply, they are:

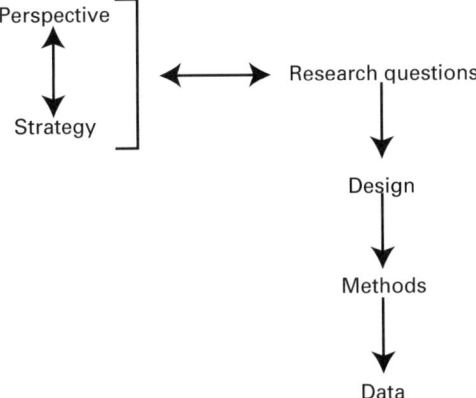

'When all of them apply' is a caveat referring to perspectives. Some research projects will start from (or be saturated with) a perspective, in which case all six components apply. But equally, many projects take the pragmatic position of questions requiring answers, in which case the five components (strategy, research questions, design, methods and data) will apply. In these cases, a perspective is implicit rather than explicit. Sometimes, too, a perspective which is implicit at the start of a project may become much more explicit during the project.

Appendix 2: Questions to Guide Proposal Development

This appendix brings together the questions raised in earlier chapters. Together, they constitute a comprehensive checklist of questions to help students in proposal development. They are of three types.

First, there are the questions about the context for the proposal noted in Chapter 2:

- Who will read my proposal?
- What will their expectations be?
- What is the process for approval of my proposal?
- What departmental and/or university guidelines are there for my proposal and its presentation?

Second, there are the three general and overarching questions highlighted in Chapter 3:

- *What* – What is my research about?
  – What is its purpose?
  – What is it trying to find out or achieve?
  and especially
  – What questions is it trying to answer?
- *How* – How will my research answer its questions?
- *Why* – Why is this research worth doing?
  – What is the significance and contribution of my study?

Third, there is a set of middle range questions to help in proposal development. I call them 'middle range' questions because they sit between the general overarching questions above, and the many, much more specific and technical questions which can be asked of research. These specific and detailed questions were presented in Chapter 12 of *Introduction to Social Research* (Punch, 1998), and concern such technical details as the internal validity of the research design, or the reliability and validity of the data, or aspects of data collection or analysis methods. While they are sometimes appropriate questions to ask of proposals, these detailed questions are generally more applicable to completed projects and reports.

The following list brings together the questions from Chapters 3, 4 and 5. Naturally, there is some overlap between them, and this list consolidates and summarizes them. The more detailed versions of some of the questions can be consulted in the review sections at the end of Chapters 3, 4 and 5.

Checklist questions to help in proposal development

Area, Topic, Purpose

1. What is my research area? Have I clearly identified it?
2. What is my topic? Have I clearly identified it, and shown how it fits within the research area?
3. What is the overall purpose of my research?

Background and Context

4. Into what background and context does my research fit?

Research Questions

5. What are my general research questions?
6. What are my specific research questions?
7. Does each specific research question meet the empirical criterion? That is, is it clear what data are required to answer each question?

Relevant Literature

8. What literature is relevant to my study?
9. What is the relationship of my study to this literature?
10. How will my study deal with the literature?
11. How does my proposal use the literature?

Perspective

12 Is there a particular perspective behind my research?

Substantive Theory

13. What is the role of theory in my study?
    – Does the description–explanation distinction apply? If my purpose is explanatory, is the focus on theory generation or theory verification? What is the logic behind my position?
    – Does the theory-generation–theory-verification distinction apply? What is the logic behind my position?
    – If my focus is theory verification, what are the hypotheses and what is the theory behind them?

Pre-structured versus unfolding

14. To what extent is my study pre-structured or unfolding? Does this apply differentially to different parts of my study?

Methods and data

15. Will my study use quantitative methods and data, qualitative methods and data, or both?
16. What strategy(ies) will my study use?
17. Does my study have a conceptual framework?
18. Who or what will be studied?
19. From whom will data be collected? Specifically, what is the sampling plan, sample size and the basis for sample selection?
20. How will I collect the data?
21. What instruments (if any) will be used? Will I use already existing instruments? If so, what is known about them? Will I develop instruments for this study? If so, using what steps?
22. What data collection procedures will be used?
23. How will these procedures maximize the quality of my data?
24. How will I analyse my data?
25. What computer packages (if any) will be involved?

Consent, Access, Ethics

26. What issues of consent are involved in carrying out my study, and how will they be dealt with?
27. What issues of access are involved in carrying out my study, and how will they be dealt with?
28. What other ethical issues are involved in carrying out my study, and how will they be dealt with?

Presentation

29. Does my proposal constitute a logical and coherent argument, with interconnected sections – do its parts fit together?
30. Have I given enough information for readers to make the judgements shown in Chapter 2 (pp. 12–13)?
31. Have I been clear? Is the proposal well organized, easy to follow and clearly written?
32. Is my proposal presented in an appropriate scholarly form?

References

Aspin, D.N. (1995) 'Logical empiricism, post-empiricism and education', in P. Higgs (ed.), *Metatheories in Philosophy of Education*. Johannesburg: Heinemann. pp. 21–49.

Behling, J.H. (1984) *Guidelines for Preparing the Research Proposal*. Revised edn. Lanham: University Press of America.

Bell, J. (1993) *Doing Your Research Project: A Guide for First Time Researchers in Education and Social Science*. 2nd edn. Buckingham: Open University Press.

Borg, W.R. and Gall, M.D. (1989) *Educational Research: An Introduction*. 2nd edn. White Plains, NY: Longman.

Bourdieu, P. (1973) 'Cultural reproduction and social reproduction', in R. Brown (ed.), *Knowledge, Education and Cultural Change*. London: Tavistock. pp. 71–112.

Brink, P.J. and Wood, M.J. (1994) *Basic Steps in Planning Nursing Research. From Question to Proposal*. 4th edn. Boston, MA: Jones and Bartlett.

Calnan, J. (1984) *Coping with Research: The Complete Guide for Beginners*. London: William Heinemann.

Campbell, J.P., Daft, R.L. and Hulin, C.L. (1982) *What to Study: Generating and Developing Research Questions*. Beverly Hills, CA: Sage.

Coley, S.M. and Scheinberg, C.A. (1990) *Proposal Writing*. Newbury Park, CA: Sage.

Creswell, J.W. (1994) *Research Design: Qualitative and Quantitative Approaches*. Thousand Oaks, CA: Sage.

Cronbach, L.J. and Suppes, P. (eds) (1969) *Research for Tomorrow's Schools: Disciplined Inquiry for Education*. New York: Macmillan.

Delamont, S., Atkinson, P. and Parry, O. (1997) *Supervising the PhD: A Guide to Success*. Buckingham: Open University Press.

Denzin, N.K. and Lincoln, Y.S. (eds) (1994) *Handbook of Qualitative Research*. Thousand Oaks, CA: Sage.

Dreher, M. (1994) 'Qualitative research methods from the reviewer's perspective', in J.M. Morse (ed.), *Critical Issues in Qualitative Research Methods*. Thousand Oaks, CA: Sage. pp. 281–97.

Durkheim, E. (1951) *Suicide: A Study in Sociology*. Trans. J. Spaulding and G. Sampson. Glencoe, IL: Free Press.

Eisner, E.W. (1991) *The Enlightened Eye: Qualitative Inquiry and the Enhancement of Educational Practice*. New York: Macmillan.

Gilpatrick, E. (1989) *Grants for Nonprofit Organizations: A Guide to Funding and Grant Writing*. New York: Praeger.

Gitlin, L.N. and Lyons, K.J. (1996) *Successful Grant Writing*. New York: Springer.

Glaser, B. (1992) *Basics of Grounded Theory Analysis*. Mill Valley, CA: Sociology Press.

Guba, E.G. and Lincoln, Y.S. (1994) 'Competing paradigms in qualitative research', in N.K. Denzin and Y.S. Lincoln (eds), *Handbook of Qualitative Research*. Thousand Oaks, CA: Sage. pp. 105–17.

Hammersley, M. (1992) 'Deconstructing the qualitative–quantitative divide', in J. Brannen (ed.), *Mixing Methods: Qualitative and Quantitative Research*. Aldershot: Avebury. pp. 39–55.

Hamper, R.J. and Baugh, L.S. (1996) *Handbook for Writing Proposals*. Lincolnwood, IL: NTC Publishing Group.

Hart, C. (1998) *Doing a Literature Review: Releasing the Social Science Research Imagination*. London: Sage.

Higgs, P. (1995) 'Metatheories in philosophy of education: Introductory overview', in P. Higgs (ed.), *Metatheories in Philosophy of Education*. Johannesburg: Heinemann. pp. 3–17.

Janesick, V.J. (1994) 'The dance of qualitative research design: metaphor, methodolatory, and meaning', in N.K. Denzin and Y.S. Lincoln (eds), *Handbook of Qualitative Research*. Thousand Oaks, CA: Sage. pp. 209–19.

Kelly, M. (1998) 'Writing a research proposal', in C. Seale (ed.), *Researching Society and Culture*. London: Sage. pp. 111–22.

Krathwohl, D.R. (1998) *Methods of Educational and Social Science Research: An Integrated Approach*. New York: Longman.

Lauffer, A. (1983) *Grantsmanship*. 2nd edn. Beverly Hills, CA: Sage.

Lauffer, A. (1984) *Grantsmanship and Fundraising*. Beverly Hills, CA: Sage.

Lefferts, R. (1982) *Getting a Grant in the 1980s*. 2nd edn. Englewood Cliffs, NJ: Prentice-Hall.

Lipsey, M.W. (1990) *Design Sensitivity*. Newbury Park, CA: Sage.

Locke, L.F., Spirduso, W.W. and Silverman, S.J. (1993) *Proposals that Work*. 3rd edn. Newbury Park, CA: Sage.

Madsen, D. (1983) *Successful Dissertations and Theses: A Guide to Graduate Student Research from Proposal to Completion*. New York: Jossey-Bass.

Marshall, C. and Rossman, G.B. (1989) *Designing Qualitative Research*. Newbury Park, CA: Sage.

Mauch, J.E. and Birch, J.W. (1989) *Guide to the Successful Thesis and Dissertation*. 2nd edn. New York: Marcel Dekker.

Maxwell, J.A. (1996) *Qualitative Research Design: An Interactive Approach*. Thousand Oaks, CA: Sage.

Maykut, P. and Morehouse, R. (1994) *Beginning Qualitative Research: A Philosophic and Practical Guide*. London: Falmer.

Meador, R. (1991) *Guidelines for Preparing Proposals*. 2nd edn. Chelsea, MI: Lewis.

Miles, M.B. and Huberman, A.M. (1994) *Qualitative Data Analysis*. 2nd edn. Thousand Oaks, CA: Sage.

Miner, L.E. and Griffith, J. (1993) *Proposal Planning and Writing*. Phoenix, AZ: Oryx.

Morse, J.M. (1994) 'Designing funded qualitative research', in N.K. Denzin and Y.S. Lincoln (eds), *Handbook of Qualitative Research*. Thousand Oaks, CA: Sage. pp. 220–35.

Moser, C.A. and Kalton, G. (1979) *Survey Methods in Social Investigation*. 2nd edn. Aldershot: Gower.

Neuman, W.L. (1994) *Social Research Methods: Qualitative and Quantitative Approaches*. 2nd edn. Boston: Allyn and Bacon.

O'Donoghue, T. and Haynes, F. (1997) *Preparing Your Thesis/Dissertation in Education: Comprehensive Guidelines.* Katoomba, NSW: Social Science Press.

Parsigian, E.K. (1996) *Proposal Savvy: Creating Successful Proposals for Media Projects.* Thousand Oaks, CA: Sage.

Peters, R.L. (1997) *Getting What You Came For: The Smart Student's Guide to Earning a Master's or a PhD.* Revised edn. New York: Noonday.

Punch, K.F. (1998) *Introduction to Social Research: Quantitative and Qualitative Approaches.* London: Sage.

Punch, M. (1994) 'Politics and ethics in qualitative research', in N.K. Denzin and Y.S. Lincoln (eds), *Handbook of Qualitative Research.* Thousand Oaks, CA: Sage. pp. 82–97.

Rosenberg, M. (1968) *The Logic of Survey Analysis.* New York: Basic Books.

Rosenthal, R. (1991) *Meta-Analytic Procedures for Social Research.* Thousand Oaks, CA: Sage.

Schofield, W. (1996) 'Survey sampling', in R. Sapsford and V. Jupp (eds), *Data Collection and Analysis.* London: Sage. pp. 25–56.

Schumacher, D. (1992) *Get Funded!* Newbury Park, CA: Sage.

Tornquist, E.M. (1993) *From Proposal to Publication: An Informal Guide to Writing About Nursing Research.* California: Addison-Wesley.

Wallen, N.E. and Fraenkel, J.R. (1991) *Educational Research: A Guide to the Process.* New York: McGraw-Hill.

Zuckerman, H. (1978) 'Theory choice and problem choice in science', in J. Gaston (ed.), *Sociology of Science.* San Francisco: Jossey-Bass. pp. 65–95.

Index